The Sword and the Rainbow

A Spiritual and Psychological Recovery from Mental Illness

by

Lynn Nackson

DORRANCE
PUBLISHING CO
EST. 1920
PITTSBURGH, PENNSYLVANIA 15238

Dorrance Publishing Co
585 Alpha Drive
Suite 103
Pittsburgh, PA 15238
Visit our website at *www.dorrancebookstore.com*

ISBN: 978-1-4809-3089-6
eISBN: 978-1-4809-3112-1

We have loved
We have had our share of strife
We have forgiven
We have loved
We have shared
This book is dedicated
To My Beloved
Jim Isenberg
My partner
My Beloved
The relationship
Like my book
Has been years now
In the making

Contents

Preface

I first met Lynn in the summer of 2013 at a Buddhist meditation group in Louisville. Our group leader mentioned that a new person coming to group was having to schedule public transportation in order to attend, and I said I'd offer this person a ride. On that first drive to group, I knew immediately that I was sitting in my car with an incredibly creative, intelligent, and interesting new friend.

Lynn was rather quick to tell me of her struggles around mental health issues. Perhaps this was her way of being authentic and forthcoming, or perhaps she wanted to defer any expectations on my part about what kind of "emotional burden" she could become, or no doubt, both.

I've found that the stigma of mental health is absorbed very deeply into the spirit those who struggle with it. For example, where the rest of us might just pass this off, Lynn is quick to apologize for some little thing she said, not wanting to offend or put someone off. However, and at the same time, her commitment to authenticity is incredibly high, and she speaks from her heart without embarrassment, even when that heart is experiencing confusion in the moment. (How many of us hold back from revealing our hearts to others during times of confusion?)

And, that's the thing… Great struggles up the ante in life. The need being so intense, they push us toward great changes in our ways of relating and being and working in the work. Such changes might involve extreme, and usually hurtful, methods of avoidance (and there are so many methods in this category available to the susceptible person.) Or they might involve deep, and often painful, spiritual work that attempts to address the very root causes of the suffering, especially when that suffering is related to "the mind", this mysterious consciousness that we as human beings seem to be uniquely equipped (or ill equipped) with. For those of us that find ourselves on the bell curve as "normal", it can be easy, at least for a time, to utilize crafty little means of denial—denial of the deep call we all have toward an experience of redemption, enlightenment, purity, oneness, health, or whatever labels one applies to that which defies labeling. For those at the fringes of that bell curve, no simple distractions will do, and one's humanness—the pain and joy of it and how to manage life's inevitable fluctuations—becomes an ultimate concern.

In Lynn, I see someone not afraid of ambiguity and groundlessness. Ok, there are times when she is very afraid as we all would be if we realized we were looking down a deep pit into… what? God knows what. What will today be like? What freak-out might happen if I go to this or that social function? What might I say to a friend in a moment of distress that will put them off forever? We all stand at the edge of that dark pit. No matter what our plans, none of us have a clue what the future will hold for us – not a future that is years head; not a future that will show up in the next 37 seconds. Those struggling with their mental health are so keenly aware of this existential ambiguity. The rest of us can act as if it ain't so, thank you very much. We can act that way at least until some event in life pulls back the tarp and we see the precariousness of where we truly stand. (Death will likely produce that tarp-pulling event for us even if nothing much happens before that.)

But, we need not fear the precariousness of living. In fact, as the great spiritual teachers say, we could embrace it. To overcome the fear of that embrace requires all we've got everything, because that "everything" is what we're holding onto to keep from falling. This is the ultimate spiritual work, I think, whether in the context of Buddhism, Christianity, any spiritual practice, and any personal growth approach. This is the work I see Lynn doing. And in having the blessing of Lynn's friendship and in the focused lens of her experience, I can see so much more clearly how I hold on, attempting to avoid the fall myself. And how close I am to that fall and the vulnerability that comes with that awareness. We should rejoice in that awareness, in any awareness, should we not? There's comfort in being asleep. But there's a time for sleep and a time for alert wakefulness ("a time to every purpose under heaven"). To taste life's richness—to experience the joy of living—requires our wakefulness, our attention, our engagement. Not a limited, selective engagement that tries to eliminate the "bad" and only connect with the "good". To practice true engagement, we have to engage it all as best we can, over, and over, and over again. Until "bad and good" no longer pull us in opposite directions. Until it all becomes simple, real, honest, open-hearted living. What else could we possibly be here for?

These spiritual lessons have become so much more apparent to me as I've explored my relationship with Lynn—through her heart, through our discussions, her descriptions of the process she's going through, the light I see in her. For Lynn, the tarp is off the pit and has been for a long time as you will see in reading her story. In reading, it might be easy to think "life is so unfair" or "there but for the grace of God go I". But Lynn's story is ultimately one of grace, hope, redemption, growth. We don't get to pick and choose our grace, you know. Scary as it might be, that's the gracefulness, the true beauty, of living.

My friendship with Lynn has and continues to nurture me in my own personal walk through life, with all its blind stumbles and small successes. Thank you, Lynn, for that nurturing. I look forward to many more years together as friends, Grace be willing.

—Stuart Braune, December, 2015

Introduction

Everyone has a life story that can be told in a way that brings enlightenment to the reader. We share the same thoughts and feelings that have led us as a human race down the path that is an evolution we call the history of humanity. This particular story is mine; it is a story of achievement and failure, of suffering and joy. There, is in my story, violence in my childhood, but there is also great faith, even in my childhood, that I would be led through any experience to a higher level as a spiritual being, loved by God, and somehow the chaos and uncertainty would pass, as all experiences do. In my story there are also times when I was physically assaulted, sexually abused, and emotionally traumatized. Most significantly to my story is my suffering with a severe and persistent mental illness from which I am recovering. This illness has led to years of institutionalization, being restrained to a bed for days at a time, and the administration of drugs that turned my thoughts into a mindless haze and even an incident of professional rape.

I started this book years ago as a record of my suffering. As I grew over a couple of decades, I saw the importance was not how much I suffered, or how intensely I suffered, but what I have learned through both pleasure and pain. I gave a great deal of thought to what I wanted to accomplish in writing this piece of creative nonfiction, describing my voyage through the dark night of my mental illness. As I reflected on what had been wasted, I cried tears of grief. As I saw what had been gained, I cried tears of joy. My beliefs about reality are a rainbow of colors—many distinct colors—blended together. I give thanks to my God for the gifts of faith and hope that led through the storm to an outlook that all phenomena in our human experience are impermanent. What is permanent is the God that leads the part of us that cannot be touched through the dangers of this diverse terrain. Surely Noah, after suffering the agony of the flood, looked from his perspective at the glorious promise of God as it was demonstrated by the rainbow, and in awe thanked the god that had spared his life.

These are selected moments of how I have reconciled the various experiences of life with a belief in a Creator, who allows the floods, allows the joy and delight, allows phenomena to unfold in an ever changing drama and allows all manner of great suffering and redemption. The rainbow appears at unusual times in this story. It reminds me that I am learning to live fully every day of my life, in spite of symptoms of illness and poverty. Eventually, it showed me how even events that were catastrophic, have led me to take responsible action for my life. Phenomena such as loss of loved ones, or loss of a way of life we considered comfortable, are often what make us check and perhaps change our values and our perspective of what is real and what is a mere delusion. The Buddha, in the *Dammapada*, describes the delusional thoughts as painted chariots passing by. Delusional does not refer to thinking of oneself as God, or thinking that someone is "out to get you" in the sense used in the mental health profession; delusions are the misperceptions we have about the importance or significance of everyday experience. We grasp for what is harmful to us, hoping to relieve the pain and suffering that is an inevitable part of life. We will always have pain, but there is an answer to suffering.

Often blessings make us grateful and joyful, but I do believe that pain is our greatest teacher. We do not have to look for it; it finds us as surely as our shadow. It is the sword into whose point we are constantly falling. It is the point that splits the road we take. The sword is the making of the tough decision to build an ark in the face of ridicule. It is the tough decision to say "no" to a way of life that, time after time, has led to the stab of reality and the shattering of a system or belief that has caused us great suffering. Too often we have stubbornly held onto what we thought was bringing us great pleasure, or at least a place of safety, that we find is merely a diversion from the route that would bring us peace and equanimity. The sword is the decision that makes the delineation between great suffering and a calm mind. The split in the road often calls for us to take the difficult path; the difficult path almost invariably is the one that, at the end of the day, has the lightest burden. We are constantly falling into the future. Sometimes painful, the point of the sword; sometimes, though, especially with the perspective of time, we find it delightful.

I can look back at times when I have chosen a way of thinking or acting that led to grave consequences. Disastrous consequences. Consequences that could have taken my life in my prime. My illness certainly affected my decisions, but my choices led me to hell. Some of my choices have brought me to fulfillment.

Of course, I am not a soothsayer. I cannot say what would have happened if I had turned to the left or to the right. I did not have the understanding of life at seventeen that I do at sixty-five. But, after repeating the same choices a multitude of times and getting slapped to the ground time after time, I finally began to wonder, "Is this really a place of safety? The institution? Is this hatred of myself truly justified? Is there, in fact, a place of safety?"

The rainbow and the sword are both perceived from within. This sword—this choice in front of us—is always pointed at ourselves. Each person has different circumstances, different biological factors, and an expansion within that is as large as the universe beyond. It *is* a universe. Each person is faced with a sword that is both alike and different than any other person's on this planet. The more aware we are of that sword and the choices delineated by that sword, the more conscious can be our decisions. We can choose the way pointed to the rainbow, or surely the sword will point to our folly.

madness

madness combs the hair on its arms
feeds corpses before they are raised from the dead
   sits in the doll's teacup

                              the promised land
   in perpetual pout
                        among the morning glories

parachutes come quietly near
                     like priests

and disappear in the white of an eye

Chapter One

The State Mental Hospital, 1968

The old building loomed at the top of the hill. It was a massive building with large screened windows with bars. I could see through the windshield of the paddy wagon that the trees were bare this early winter day, with their arms lifted up as though crying to the heavens. I was too drained from weeping at this point to plead for the mercy for which the trees seemed to beg. It was my destiny now. I seemed to be a helpless child of the State. Perhaps it became my destiny when I took that first overdose on aspirin in the university dorm. All effort at that time had been made by my roommate and her sorority big sister to conceal what was the first domino to have fallen.

Could it have stopped this drama, which at the moment seemed to be the end of some Shakespearian tragedy? At what point, if any, was the choice made? I was brought to the state hospital from Highland Baptist, a private psychiatric unit that no longer exists. Whenever possible, I had inflicted dreadful wounds upon myself, obsessively.

"If you don't stop this self-destructive behavior," my psychiatrist informed me, "you will end up in a state mental hospital."

In the private hospital I had lost conception of what was "normal" behavior. I was in a cycle I did not know how to stop. I knew something was very wrong with my life, and I was desperate to fix it. I was not finding answers here. Little guidance was given on how to resist the horrid feeling of wanting to inflict injury on myself, and I couldn't imagine ever leaving the presumed

1

safety of the hospital unit. It was like being in a small boat in the ocean without even a compass.

The day I left for the state hospital seemed like a particularly calm day on the unit. I was working in the craft shop, engrossed in my oil painting of a farmer painting a barn green, when a nurses' aide came to the door and said, "Lynn, come with me." No one seemed to pay attention to what was a common occurrence. It could be my psychiatrist was making his rounds, which was usually the most significant five to fifteen minutes of the patient's day. The life buoy would be thrown out, only to disappear as soon as the swimmer reached it. The group in the craft room paid little attention to who came and went. There were glazed salad bowls and teapots, salt and pepper shakers in the form of Santa's elves, miniature Christmas trees complete with tiny lights, and all kinds of seasonal ceramics that were painted and fired. This era in psychiatric hospitalization focused on soothing activities to manage the patients. Recovery was not the goal in psychiatric treatment; maintenance was. Also, the use of the craft room was often a reward for acceptable behavior.

When the aide shut the door behind me, I saw a small brown suitcase in her hand that I did not recognize as mine.

"Where are we going?" I asked, my gut feeling as someone had deflated it.

"You are going to the state hospital," she answered without emotion.

Everything in my range of vision was shaking like someone was rattling my head. I was whimpering, but had known, though I denied it, that this was inevitable considering I could not seem to control the desire to destroy myself. I had moved from simple acts of self-harm to outright suicide attempts. I followed the aide down the hallway to a locked metal door, which I had never seen used before. It was useless to resist. A patient never won in a physical altercation. She rattled some keys to open the door, and then the door slammed behind me.

Down the staircase to the parking lot I walked, not knowing what to expect. There, waiting, was a paddy wagon with a uniformed policewoman here for her delivery. She opened the double doors and indicated with a movement of her hand that I was to get in. All in a day's work.

As I looked in at my fellow representatives of the population of those considered incompetent to live in society at large, I said to myself, "This can't be." I knew I was expected to take my place beside the four other patients being transported, but was unable to take that step into the transportation for the insane.

"Load up, honey. I ain't got all day." The policewoman spoke without impatience, but, instead, had a rather kindness in her tone.

The garb of my compadres reflected my new identity. I was the one out of style. I had just finished my freshman year at the university and I had been selected in my first semester as one of the ten best dressed young women on the campus. There I sat, in a burgundy cable knit sweater with matching cable knit knee highs. To my immediate right was a middle-aged woman with a navy blue suit, covered so thickly with dirt, lint, and hair that it resembled a faux fur outfit. Her white gloves were stained red. Was that blood? It had that rusty tinge to it. She looked like she had dressed for church in the fifties and remained in her clothes until now. Her outfit was completed with a "flipper" style hat with a frayed rose on her left ear and black patent leather shoes, broken with deep lines from years of use. She sat primly with her gloved hands on top of a black handbag. Her posture was flawless. Her large bosom tugged at her fake pearl buttons. She was absolutely silent, showing no signs of being distressed.

Suddenly, one of the passengers screamed, "You whores better watch out, cuz I'll bust your asses clean out of this town. You ain't gonna touch me with no dick!" She then began to mumble to herself, seemingly unaware of the other four of us that were being transported to the asylum I had never seen, never even allowed myself to imagine.

I looked at this woman, totally engaged in her own world, and wondered what her story was. She was dressed in what we used to refer to as a "house dress," that was clean and pressed. I could imagine her being in her home, dusting her ancient furniture, and being rounded up with the rest of us. There was more to the story, I was sure, but I wondered where the story began that led to her being held captive in a world that was so private, that made the world so threatening.

The wagon began moving, and I began to sob. Fear, despair, and hopelessness had been common in the last twelve months. This was not an outcome I had desired or for which I had prayed. Who gets on their knees at age five and prays that they wish to be mentally ill? This was not the future of which I had dreamed as a writer or student. There was nowhere to look for strength but inward. There seemed to exist no one but myself in this rickety truck. Everyone, including the driver and the policewoman who had herded me inside, seemed lost in some sort of vacuum. I began to feel I couldn't breathe. I calmed myself as best I could. I looked at the other two in the group. One was a young woman in jeans and a dirty tee shirt. The other was probably in her late forties or early fifties with long, stringy, dirty grey hair. She wore glasses she pushed up on her nose every few seconds. The lenses made her eyes look larger than they were. I was the only one crying. What was different in their lives that made this seem, it appeared, like something they went through on a regular basis?

We all had the same destination. These were now my peers. No longer did I have my middle class status to determine my values. The worth of each human life had suddenly become apparent to me. Each of us came here through a journey that was private, and yet the public officials saw fit to intervene. From this point forward, the man mumbling to himself on the bus, the woman standing on a street corner flailing her arm, these people I had considered derelicts, these were my peers. I wept.

"It ain't all that bad," the policewoman tried to console me from the front of the wagon.

I did not know I had any rights. They do not read them to you when you are taken away to a psychiatric facility. There is a seventy-two hour hold, which means a doctor can hold you until a court can determine if you should be committed. I knew nothing of this. I was a very naïve eighteen-year-old woman who knew nothing of the system that would both guard and threaten my life.

There was a wide mesh screen between the driver and the policewoman, and the five of us. I was not familiar with the roads on which they were taking us. We seemed to be taking the longest route, never the expressway, and with each bump in the road we were literally lifted off of our seat. I had exhausted my weeping. I sat motionless, observing the scenario as it unfolded.

Once my tears had ended, I left to a mental state where there was no emotion or conflict. It was a place to which I had gone as long as I could remember when terror grabbed me, wrapped its hands around my neck and seemed to threaten my life. It was a place as distant and as close as a fluffy white cloud on a sunny day. I floated, observing in this surreal state the reality that was grounded below me.

Until now, I had lived in a glass house. Like the window glass broken by a rock thrown by an angry child, it had shattered. Life at the university, I assumed, was over. There would not be the excitement of a date with someone with whom I started a conversation after class. There would be no more acting or backstage work in the community theatres. It was the end of languid spring days in a creative writing class, sitting in the old brick building discussing the best of students' poetry or prose with a fresh breeze cooling the room through the large open windows. The scene shifted to the lawn in front of what was then the main library on a balmy day; the albino squirrels scampered around, looking for a bite of a French fried potato or a piece of bread, perhaps left by a student's lunch. Life as I had known it was over. I was, I felt, a prisoner with no chance for parole. To me, institutionalization was the end.

We took a sharp left, all leaning on one another for support. I snapped to the present. Whatever was to come, I believed at that point I could not control it. No longer did I feel desperate. I could not feel panic. It was resignation. It was the most solemn moment of my life, as I had yet experienced it. It was looming ahead. It was there. The institution. The paddy wagon pulled up to the main entrance with large round white columns and a concrete porch. This enormous building would devour me.

After we stopped, the policewoman came with nothing akin to a rush to the back of the vehicle. She took out her jangling batch of keys and thumbed through them until she found the one that fit. She worked for a few seconds with the lock, and pulled the doors apart. "Okay, ladies," she said as though she had said this thousands of times before, "let's go. We're here."

"You don't gotta drag me out of this here Cadillac," the verbal leader of our clan proclaimed.

We followed her down the step from the wagon to the ground. Apparently, I was the only one with luggage, because the police officer had only in her hand that brown suitcase which followed me from the psychiatric unit. We went in front of her up the steps into a foyer with high ceilings and a cracked marble floor, which could have easily been the entrance into an age old courthouse. A guard in uniform greeted us in the foyer.

"You need anything more, Anna?" the driver asked.

"No," she answered, "I'll see you in a while."

"Harry here is a good guy. He'll take care of you." He turned and headed back to the vehicle.

We were led from one austere environment to an even more oppressive room off to the side with wooden benches lining the blank walls. The room was probably originally white, but had been stained to a dingy yellow from years of accumulated nicotine. The room had evidently housed many people over the years, perhaps like myself, waiting for what they did not know would be next. Nomads, we were. Going from nowhere to nowhere. It made little difference. Being moved from one hell to the next was hardly an improvement. Yet, I did not fantasize about what might be the next torturous moment, only the sense that one feels when there is no choice left. The item for which one so desperately has been looking is, indeed, lost. I had some sort of dismal peace about no longer fearing what could happen, for it had happened. I sat motionless, but began to survey the environment, Anna, Harry, and my peers. The smell of body odor and stale urine brought to mind a cattle car passing by as I sat in an old sedan with the windows rolled down. Not all of the group was motionless. The young woman and the verbally active woman rocked back and forth. I would eventually discover the self-soothing nature of this rhythmical movement.

"Give me a cigarette, Anna," demanded the verbal rocker.

"That is not the way to get something," Anna retorted. Yet she, without seeming to begrudge her, handed her a cigarette she pulled from her breast pocket. She took one for herself. As she lit up, the patient walked to the wall. I saw for the first time the maximum security lighter on the wall. She pushed a button, and a small grid lit up bright red. The smell of tobacco made the noxious odor already saturating the room even more nauseating. I watched the smoker purse her lips as she inhaled, smoke coming out of her nose, followed by a hacking cough.

I wondered, *What makes a room turn into a hell? Did these walls house those sentenced to cleanse their sins?* It was simply a hell because I desired more. I did not even know what it was I desired. It was not just a more pleasant environment. All of us have been places we did not care to be. It was a desire for a life that offered satisfaction more than a desire for success. I doubted I would be able to succeed or find satisfaction in this environment, whatever my destiny here.

"Anna!" the smoker addressed the policewoman as though they had known each other for years. "Anna! I wanna pop!"

"You'll get something to drink when you are admitted," Anna said indifferently. "You know the routine."

You know the routine, I mused. Evidently, she had left and come back. I wondered if that was a common occurrence. Left and came back. Left. I had assumed this was a permanent residence.

We, waiting, did not acknowledge the others detained here. There were no words shared. Perhaps the others were also self-absorbed. Did they even know where they were? I was too weary to even ask questions, if, in fact, these women were willing to talk. I was curious about what brought them here. What happened to you? Have you been here before? The wait was growing long; the isolation only intensified.

Finally, the significant rattling of the keys. The door opened. I felt a sudden racing of my heart. Perhaps there was life still in my body. A slight, short man in a grey suit with a red bow-tie entered and paused, surveying the group.

"Line them up," he spoke in an accent I could not discern—probably French.

The smoker hurried to be the first in line. I wanted, above all, not to do anything wrong in order to prevent any wrath from being directed at me, but I could not move out of my fear and lack of understanding of the process.

"Sara, you want to go to D2? You fell, as they say, off of the wagon. Eez that right?"

"I wanna pop," she answered with a statement.

"Pateence! Pateence! Please, where is Transportation? How can I admeet without transportation?"

Anna pulled out her radio and called, requesting Transportation to come to the holding room. Noticing me sitting on the bench, he walked to me and introduced himself. "I am Dr. Potts. Are you eighteen or over? (I always looked younger than my age. I was five feet, three inches tall, and weighed only a few pounds over a hundred. I wore my hair short, and was often told I looked quite innocent.) Yes, you must be Lynn Campbell. Received a call from your doctor today. Ah, so there are bandages on your wreest. You will come to my floor. L7."

"Who is theese?" he asked Anna. Harry was disregarding the whole process, standing with his foot on the bench, smoking.

"Her name is Irene Black. She was found sitting on a bench in Central Park." They were speaking of the woman in the navy faux fur suit. "At least, we think she is Irene Black. Had some opened letters addressed to her. She won't speak, but does exactly as she is told."

"Are you Irene Black?" the doctor directed a question at her.

Surprisingly, she answered softly, "Yes, Sir."

"She eez scared. Seend her to S1."

He stopped the interrogation to write a few notes. Transportation arrived. Two male guards in their brown uniforms. "Take theese one first," he ordered, indicating me with a nod. "She eez going to L7. Tell them to take all precautions. I weel be up shortly to write the orders."

"I wanna go to the canteen," popped Sara.

I did not hear their response for one of the guards hustled me out of the door. I had learned quite a bit in the holding room. People came and went. There was a canteen. There were different units for different purposes. Apparently, those women, like myself, who were considered dangerous to themselves, or perhaps others, were kept on L7.

It was a long walk, it seemed, through locked doors, each requiring jumbling keys. We reached a rickety, clanging elevator and the guard pushed the number three. The smell of urine was even stronger. I noticed a suspicious puddle in the corner of the elevator. We creaked up several floors and there was yet another hall with dirty green and once white linoleum. The hallway was light, though, for the large barred windows let in the sun of this clear day. But, I did not have a coat, and the halls were cold and unwelcoming.

"This way, Hon," the guard informed me indicating yet another metal door and more clanging of the keys.

This was apparently the destination of this lengthy admission to this state mental hospital. Here was where the winding road ended. The guard opened the door, and I saw a long hallway. To my left was a series of doorways with no doors. I could see the first room had four beds that were arranged against the square shape of the room. Yellowish orange bricks made up the walls. The beds were made up neatly with blankets that resembled the blankets my father had been issued in the service in World War II. My mother had always packed these deep green thin blankets for me to take to summer camp, Where was my father now? He obviously had agreed to my confinement here. I could remember no discussion with him about this, but Highland Baptist was fading in my memory now. What I could remember seemed to have no bearing on this moment. It was a blacked out script on a manuscript someone who I had never met had written. It was gone. I was becoming enmeshed in the moment.

To my right was a long counter, a nurses' station, obviously. All the nurses and aides were in white uniforms. A nurse with two stripes on her cap, indicating she was an RN, approached us.

"What have we got here?"

"Umm … an eighteen year old girl. Take all precautions. Doc says he will write the orders shortly."

"Okay. She goes in in the first room, bed two. Jenny, get her cleaned up," she ordered another woman without a cap, evidently an aide.

I stared at the austere surroundings. There were women in grey gowns wandering in and out of the doorless doorways, but most of them were in a room at the far end of the hall.

A woman walked with long, fast strides, up and down the hallway, screeching and laughing, clearly in another plane than I. Another was moving slowly down the hallway with her arms bent at the elbow. She looked incredibly stiff and scooted down the hall without lifting her feet. No one had shoes, but all wore beige sock slippers that are issued in hospitals. All had on grey gowns coming half way down their legs, short sleeves, a large round neckline, and a lack of buttons or snaps.

I couldn't figure out why I had to get cleaned up. I always showered in the evening. Still, I dutifully went with the aide. Half way down the row of doors there was a door leading to the shower room. What I saw appalled me. There was a row of shower heads on one side and a row of seatless toilets on the left. There were no stalls or shower curtains. The shower room smelled as though it had been collecting human waste since the hospital opened. How many people had been in my position? There was a pile of human feces just past my feet, laying ignored on the floor. Jenny accepted it with all the other furnishings of this room that offered no modesty. The aide began rummaging through my short hair, and said, more to herself than me, "No lice."

I was trying, somehow, to make this into a story that had a foreseeable ending. But, as far as I knew, this was the story and this was it. The people talked about me as though I were a piece of furniture. I did not know what they wanted or what to expect. ."Here's some shampoo and soap," she said, handing a single bottle of liquid soap. Well," she added, "get in the shower. I ain't got all day."

I was very self-conscious about my slight build and small breasts. Some of my friends had called me "Twiggy." You would have had to grown up in the

9

era I did to understand my reference to this petite model. I did not want to take off my clothes in front of a gawking person, even if it was a woman. A memory flashed about something . . . some shame about my body . . . but it disappeared before it was fully in my conscious mind.

The water was cold. I was afraid to look for any way of adjusting the temperature. I just wanted to be left alone somewhere, where I could begin to reflect on what was happening to me. I had never been in jail. This seemed to be what this was. I shampooed my hair and washed my body with great care, so as not to appear to Jenny as anything but compliant. Eventually, she was satisfied and handed me one small white towel. I was given one of the patient uniforms I had seen on all my other peers.

After the shower was complete, Jenny showed me where I would sleep. My bed was against the wall, first bed on the left, in full view of the nurses' station. "This is where you'll sleep. We ain't a hotel. You are up at six every morning and showered by the time I get here at seven." Jenny then marched out of the room, and the tears that had stopped started once again.

"She's going off!" the RN proclaimed.

Three aides appeared, and I was rushed down the hall to a thick wooden door with a square small glass window that had mesh in the unbreakable heavy pane. I was stripped of everything, and the door shut; the keys told me the door was locked.

I was not surprised at this point at what I saw. A metal bunk, and a metal drain in the center of the floor. I stood, looking, and wondered what I was supposed to do. What could I do? I had not used the restroom since I had left Highland. Warm urine made its way down my bare legs. I could not stop it. The puddle I made found its way to the drain. *Gee*, I thought, *they think of everything*. I felt tremendous relief at having emptied my bladder.

I sat on the edge of the cold metal bunk, once again in silence. I sat looking at my surroundings. The walls were like the rest of the unit—rusty yellow bricks. The high ceiling had a bulb covered with a stained plastic cover. I assumed the light was always on. I could hear occasional muffled voices as patients and staff made their way down the hall, but I could not make out any specific words. The metal bunk was beginning to warm beneath my buttocks and thighs.

Resigned to be here for an undetermined time, I lay down on the bunk. My thoughts took me away, years away. To the sixth grade in my hometown.

My friend Anne and I would take walks every day when we got home from school. The large old homes in this section of town had plenty of yard room for "Kick the Can" or "Mother May I?" The entire neighborhood would play on summer nights. Our walk would take us a few blocks, past the houses, to a hill overlooking other hills, which were higher in the distance. We would walk and sit in cold or heat, rain or snow. We would sit for half an hour or an hour and meditate on the wind or the changes the seasons had made. No one but the two of us ever appeared here. It was where we prayed, where we wondered about what was to be. It was not a place we talked or giggled; it was a place of deep reverence. I was not on the bunk anymore. I was there, in the thick woods, in Nature, thanking God for my life, not aware of the hospital, or what seemed to be its horrors. I was a child again, dreaming of when I would have my own child, and how I would raise the child to appreciate the sounds whispering from what I felt to be Heaven. The smell of rain in the spring. The glory of autumn as the trees rallied to their winter sleep. How much beauty and peace in this natural green cathedral was just beyond my grasp right now.

Suddenly, I heard the keys and the door opened. A woman without a cap held a gown in her hand. "Come on, Honey. Everyone is in the dayroom. They are handing out cigarettes."

I did not smoke, but was relieved to be covered and relatively free. The shift must have changed because I had not seen this woman earlier. Her kindness made me want to cry, but I quickly stifled the impulse. Confinement within confinement. This was the consequence of fear, of despair.

At the end of the hall was the dayroom. My first impression was that it reminded me of our old high school cafeteria. But the tables and chairs were quite heavy, probably because they were not easily picked up and thrown. Age old windows, much larger than modern buildings, had screens locked with padlocks.

The uniformed patients were formed into two lines. In one line the patients waited for two generic cigarettes. The second line was for the lighter on the wall. Although I did not want the cigarettes, I stood in line because I did not want to stand out from the rest of the crowd. I did not know quite what to do with the cigarettes. Just hid them in my fist and walked to my seat

For a few minutes the patients seemed quite content. I felt quite obvious with my cigarettes under my hand, seated at the table. I watched as the women inhaled. Their eyes seemed glazed, and they had a distant, dreamy look as though they had escaped the environment. An aide, smoking with the patients, had that same glazed, distant look.

"Hey," a toothless lady sitting next to me said in a whisper, looking furtively around as she spoke, "don't you want them cigarettes? Give 'em to me. Don't tell no one cuz we'll both end up in Seclusion."

My mother had always said wanting a cigarette was like wanting water in the desert. I had begged her to quit, but she always dismissed me with "Oh, Lynn, I am not going to die of lung cancer. "

I decided I had to get rid of the cigarettes, so I slid them to the woman. "I owe you, Baby," she expressed with gratitude.

Two of the women in the front row of tables were mischievously whispering and laughing. It was obvious they wanted no one to hear what they were saying for they glanced around, surveying all the audience around. A lot of secrets were exchanged in this seemingly still forest of tree trunks. I wondered how those two could find it in themselves to laugh with the Keepers ever watching, ever listening. No one else was talking, except those mumbling to themselves. In some ways it was like being held in detention after school.

For now, I was very much in the moment. This was my life. It was as though nothing, nowhere else, existed. I sat with everyone else waiting. Waiting for what? I became aware of a steady tick in the background. It was an institutional clock marking every second. It seemed like many, many hours since I had walked onto this unit, but it was only late afternoon.

Then my own private entertainment began. A male choir, like, perhaps what would occur in a monastery. I had heard this choir many times before, but had become aware that it was not audible to anyone other than myself. I could never make out the words. They came from the walls. Sometimes the choir was there. Sometimes it was not. I was careful not to acknowledge its presence in any way. I caught myself rocking back and forth as I listened, but quickly stopped myself. I had an idea that on this unit absolutely anything was the norm, but I did not want to show I had symptoms in common with my peers. The soothing chanting abruptly came to a stop. Two middle-aged women began fighting, pulling hair and scratching like two cats gone at each other. One got shoved to the floor. I had not seen what started the altercation, but at the same time another incident began between two women at the end of the first row of chairs."MANPOWER EMERGENCY, L7. MANPOWER EMERGENCY L7." A loud voice instantaneously came on over the intercom. This undoubtedly was the State Hospital protocol for getting help to a unit where there was a behavioral disturbance.

The second affront was verbal. From my right a woman with long scraggly grey hair and a crisp face that looked as though it had seen a lot of weather approached a woman sitting in a chair to my left.

"I know you stole my husband! I love Tammy, but you better stay away from my husband!" She held a Bible in front of her and screeched, "Touch it! Touch it!"

Meanwhile, Manpower had almost without a ripple in time removed the first offenders. The Keepers were confronting the woman who loved Tammy to get in her seat or be taken with the others to Seclusion. *How many Seclusion rooms were on the unit?*

The woman accused of stealing her husband said in an amazingly calm voice, "What, are you *crazy?*"

The Keeper took Tammy's lover by the arm, and she allowed herself to be led to her chair and sat, obviously agitated and uttering obscenities at no one in particular. *Interesting, I observed, the hierarchy of insanity. One of the madwomen considers Tammy crazy, a clear distinction from what she obviously thinks of herself.*

Everyone, including the staff, reacted as indifferently as if a motorcycle had passed by while driving down the highway. I was learning, as I had learned boarding the paddy wagon, to the Keepers it was all in a day's work. Emotion was to be held in captivity. I remembered my mother's habit of reading the obituaries aloud at the breakfast table. In a flat voice she would announce, "Ole Miss Janice died. They found nine cats in her house. Wonder what they will do with them." It was all in a day in a small town. Someone was born. Someone died. Another day. Not much else to talk about. In this grim scene on the floor that was evidently for those high in the hierarchy of the mentally ill. It was becoming normal very rapidly to me. I was not terrified of anything external at this point. I was terrified of the voices that were screaming at me. Voices that only came when something in me felt threatened. This was part of my secret life. I had spoken to no one, here or anywhere, about it. Especially those here who made it known their power could not be challenged.

Even in the private hospital, my psychiatrist quickly let it be known that not I, nor any of the patients, could not get inside his skin or any of the rest of the staff, much less disrupt the peace of the unit. The only one I could harm was myself. His presence was absent here. I could never discuss the real fears, the fear of being cut off, of being looked at with disdain. I could not piece together the relationship of my abuse from the past with the abuse against myself I used as a kind of punctuation mark for the sense of standing totally alone in life. On stage, but never applauded. But, that doctor was gone. He had no relevance here. I felt a sense of belonging at this moment that was as devoid of pain as the wrist that I had slashed without mercy. Belonging to the caste to which I was born. The private psychiatrist was now one of the ghosts of my past, that tall heavy man who scoffed whenever I spoke. Because I had received shock treatments, ECT there, and the shock of the transfer to a barred institution, it would be a long time before I could put together the experiences, the jagged twists and turns that lead to this sparsely furnished room. The shock treatments were over, anyway. I didn't have to be put through that sudden death, as I saw it.

The relationship between behavior and consequences was muddled at this point. In many ways I was still a child. It was difficult to assess a situation, difficult to evaluate impulses, and difficult to determine what actions to take. I could not imagine where I would be in a year. Even at the university, I had no real sense of what direction I wanted my life to take. I did not know what it was that I wanted. Here, on this unit, I had a bed and a gown. I had my peers and those whose purpose was to control us. Keep us in line. Keep us walking, sitting, and lying down. The Keepers.

As the room settled down, the shouting voices faded into the muffled sound effects of the insane. Sudden outcries without obvious cause. Muddled rumblings from those caught in their own hell. I had no everyday decisions to make-like whether to do the laundry or make a phone call. There were no decisions and few choices. I only waited with my peers for the Keepers to make the next directional lead

My thinking was directed at survival, unlike the secret motives that often directed my actions. As a younger teenager, I had referred to myself as a chameleon, fitting in with any crowd in any situation. Yet, not truly fitting in anywhere. To be an "outsider" was truly to be an "insider." Inside my own head, without thinking of what others might need from me. My motive was to get a word of understanding, of approval. I had found through my creative writing, primarily poetry, a way to gather applause. It became my main method of honest communication. I could not think of myself as a person who was worthy for just who I was. Often, I would reflect in private on some casual comment I had made and cover my face with my hands, saying, "Oh, I'm so dumb and stupid!" I would agonize over even the simplest interaction.

"Dinner!" one of the aides announced as a food cart was rolled into the room. "Line up!" Everyone was particularly interested in the arrival of food, but I saw it as just a break in the blessed monotony of endless waiting for ....? Compulsively, I looked at the clock. Five-thirty. Same time we had dinner at home.

Still, I was in no rush to eat. I never had much of an appetite, picked at my food, and the severe emotional drain of the day left me longing only to find a comfortable place where I could lay my head, withdrawn from the world as I now knew it. I moved to the back of the line to draw out this diversion as long as possible.

Dinner consisted of three servings that could only be distinguished from one another by a slightly different yellowish grey color. In my mind it looked like someone had vomited in each of the three sections of the plastic tray and left a lumpy mush. My instinct was to drop the tray, but one episode in seclusion had taught me the value of self-control. I took my tray to my seat and played with my food with the plastic spoon, which was the only utensil given. I wanted to appear I was eating this noxious concoction.

Supper was finished and the trays were stacked and taken out. Then there was another round of cigarettes with no disturbances. After each wandering of my thoughts, I would check the clock. I would try to see how long I could go without obsessively watching every five minutes pass. It became a game. I was waiting for bedtime, though the thought of sleeping on this unit was frightening.

I observed some of the behavior around me to distract myself. A woman was combing the hair on her arms with a plastic comb. Many of the patients were mumbling to themselves, and occasionally someone would shout something that could not be related to the present situation, at least as I perceived it. It made me wonder if anyone's perception of reality was truly accurate. If three people looked at an object; there were three different perspectives.

Furthermore, there would be a whole different long string of associations to that object. Some of them were associations, or conditions, one had chosen. Some had been inflicted upon the one who perceived the object. I suppose my perception of I how I ended in this environment was as accurate as any psychiatrist, clinical social worker, psychologist or psychiatric nurse could interpret it. If, in the past, I perceived that I had succeeded—at making a high grade in school or winning an award, it was simply because the conditions had been right for me to make that achievement. I did not *choose* to succeed or not succeed. There were the conditions at that time to succeed. I chose the object of my success on the basis of all conditions, all objects of my life until that moment. These people around me—now and in the past—could not begin to understand my own personal universe—indeed universes upon universes—that existed only in my own mind. The objects I perceived were the objects of my own mind. Nowhere in my past moments had I been more aware of my own mind than here, in this moment. And, I came to accept, in this moment, that I was here simply because the conditions had been there for me to end up in this place, at this time.

I needed to use the restroom. No one had left the dayroom in the last few minutes; perhaps I could have some privacy. I used the toilet as hurriedly as possible and ambled back to the dayroom. I observed a row of seclusion rooms. Yes, they were prepared. Would it be possible to develop a dependency on *this* institution? How did people actually get out of here? As I entered the dayroom, I glanced at the clock. Six-fifty-two.

I was incredibly tired. The hard chairs were so uncomfortable. I would make a point of using the restroom every hour to break up the discomfort. There was not even a television here.

Seven thirty. More cigarettes. This time I did not bother to get in the line. I did not want to risk getting caught passing my generous allotment to someone else. I relaxed a bit, hearing the choir of soothing voices. I was oblivious to the ravages of psychosis around me. I felt serene.

"Give me my cigarette butt!" an angry patient demanded to the woman on her right. I snapped to my present environment

"What are you talking about? I don't have your damn cigarette butt!"

"Yes you do! It was lying right here! I didn't smoke it! You got it!"

"Where do you think I'm hiding it? Up my crotch?"

I was wondering if Security would be called, but the woman without her butt sat back down, talking to herself and looking around on the floor for the prized item. The accused folded her arms and leaned back, content that she had the upper hand. In a way, I was disappointed the conflict had ended in such a benign fashion, for a disruption would have at least have broken the incessant ticking of the clock, the red hand in distinct, separate movements against its white background with black numbers.

It was now almost nine o'clock. I waited for the next interruption, took another walk to the restroom, and began to expect that there would be some marking of bedtime. Surely, we would be medicated. I was certain our sleep was as desirable for our Keepers as much as for ourselves. Sure enough, an aide came to the door and made the proclamation, for which I was waiting. "Ladies, it's time for bedtime meds. Line up at the nurses' station."

There was no admonishing necessary. Some of the more aggressive patients shoved their way to the front of the line. I lingered behind, unsure of whether I had been prescribed medication.

"Who is this?" the nurse with two stripes on her hat asked

"Campbell, new today."

I was the new project.

"The doctor has ordered you Thorazine," explained the nurse.

She handed me a medicine cup filled with a thick orange syrup. It tasted incredibly vile and bitter. I squelched an automatic gag, which made one of the Keepers chuckle.

Within minutes, my brain felt like cotton, and I had difficulty finding my way to my bed. I lay my head on the plastic pillow, and soon I was overtaken by a "sliver of death," as Poe called it, a deep, dreamless sleep. And, the day and the evening were the first day. As is said in Genesis.

somehow

somehow
wanting to possess
the magic
in this blue glass
blown shapely,
I found it did possess
my hand
and swallowed
and I was it

and finding an old toy chest
labeled "People"
I put on old clothes
and paper hats
and reaped,
and reaped
a harvesting of applause
which is
silence
that drank
and I was it

and well
(we say)
that's life
and I am it

a drink of water
in an open hand

Chapter Two

Blue Glass Blown Shapely

It is difficult to determine whether mental illness is environmental, biological, or both. Some illnesses clearly seem to be biological, while others are not understood. One thing is for sure, those of us who deal with a severe and persistent illness did not request it, and do not want it. Three things the mentally ill deal with are stigma, symptoms, and self-image. Often the symptoms are hidden because of the stigma, and the self-image is affected by both the symptoms and the stigma. It is a merry-go-round that often exists before it is known that so does the illness. I know I had many psychological issues as a child.

I suspect my childhood in western Kentucky appeared to the small population to be like any other part of the progression of life in the community. In many ways I excelled. There was a troubled period in school for a year or so, but those in authority in the school system, I believe, thought that was a "phase." It was rectified with "proper discipline." My best friend at the time and I cut a class—the apex of my rebellious period—and spent two weeks in after school detention.

Life in our perceived microcosm of society was in many ways slow paced and bountiful. As a child, the whole neighborhood of children often played childhood games together outside and barefoot. One of the boys had a complex tree house his father had built, but there was clearly written in crayon on crumpled white paper the notification that "no girls were allowed." However, on one quiet Saturday afternoon, my friend Anne and I managed to sneak into this wonderful hide away without the proper credentials.

There was a Strawberry Festival in late spring that had nothing to do with strawberries. There would be cotton candy and roasted hot dogs. There were never any strawberries anywhere on Main Street where the festival was held. Most of the small shops were on Main Street. A typically stately county court house was at the center of the town which took great pride in their cordial Southern heritage. At this, the most important day uptown for children on this small town street in the fifties, there was a Ferris wheel that had a very high top. Well, it was a very high top to those of us who had attended no other fair or even an amusement parks outside of our own county. One year a friend and I were on the very top when the Ferris wheel broke. This merely added to our festive spirits, as we sat, seat by swinging seat, being brought to safety. There was even a "hog calling contest" in which the country women would imitate the way they would call the pigs to their slop.

As a teenager there were basketball games with homemade pizza at slumber parties in my girl friends' houses on winter Friday nights. We had lots of gossip and chiding about what boy had written us a note in class or sat next to us at lunch. There was the writing I did, which won me the Creative Writing Award upon graduation. There were Girl Scouts, sock hops, and occasionally, a good movie for a dime at the Palace Theatre. Another fifteen cents brought you a coke and popcorn.

But, in spite of the pleasantries of small town life, did anyone know what went on in the homes? What psychological scars were left in domestic disputes, even violence? One thing was for sure: emotional and mental problems were considered to be a disgrace to the family, at least in my family.

To gossip about someone who had been hospitalized from a mental disorder was done in hushed tones by the women over a cup of coffee. I remember very distinctly an obviously relished conversation between my mother and another woman that I, a child, overheard by pretending to be playing with my baby dolls in the next room, disinterested in the adult grabble.

"Did you hear about Ester?" my mother questioned her friend.

"Oh, you mean about her going to the Country Club Hospital in Louisville?" That is what they called Our Lady of Peace, or the Hospital Up on the Hill.

"Oh, yeah," my mother answered, with obvious delight, "I heard she had *shock treatments*. And she thinks she is such a hottie. She continued with even more malicious comments. "Have you seen the way she swings her legs back and forth when she is sitting?

"Yeah. I think she does that when she is nervous."

"You know what Freud called that?"

"No."

"*Masturbation!*"

"*Really?*" There was uncomfortable laughter.

My mother could not, of course, realize that at one point in her life she would be dealing with mental illness, much less the mental illness of her daughter who seemed to accomplish great things. Three children in her family, and only one diagnosed with a mental illness. Why? Would this illness bring out the shameless truths she held in denial?

We have come a long way in dispelling the shame of mental illness, but the media mostly talks about the rare incidents of violence in the mentally ill. Or, movies and literature actually glamorize or mystify it, rather than view it as a medical condition like arthritis or a broken leg. People stare at odd behavior. The same way as if someone is rolled in in a wheel chair, unable to control the movements of their limbs. Disability shows a difference, and often brings to mind fear or curiosity. Mentally ill people have the same sensitivities and emotions as any other person; their perception of reality may be different, which can cause odd behavior.

My parents divorced when I was almost four, and my mother moved back to western Kentucky to be with her parents. This required her to have an emotional and financial dependence on them that dominated the family life. Her mother was "easily upset." In truth, my mother suffered desperately, financially. She worked at the family dress shop, owned by my grandparents. Many times she would rush home from work at "the store," as we called it, frantically searching the mail for a check from our absent father for the meager child support he owed that was her legal right. She hid this from her parents. We children only saw our father at Christmas and a week or two in the summer until I was a teenager and would take a friend to visit him. To me, though for an attorney his home was modest, it was living the high life. He would take us to expensive restaurants, and we would go to real movie theatres. Eventually, upon graduation from high school, I moved to Louisville to go to college and became acquainted with my father who lived in that city.

I have few memories of what life was like when my parents were married. I remember a violent argument between my mother and father about the time of the divorce. I awakened to screaming and peaked around the corner of my bedroom. My father had his hands around my mother's throat.

"Give me that thing!" Dad ordered in a coarse voice about something I could not see.

"No, no!" my mother whimpered in a very small voice.

"Get back in your bed!" my father yelled at me, noticing me as I watched in horror.

I ran to my bed, and buried my head in my pillow. I was afraid I would be hit. I was afraid my parents would hit each other. Mother ran in and threw herself on top of me. "I am going to take you away from that awful man," she whispered to me. I remember hating her for that.

From here this part of my life is very hazy. I do not actually remember the move to western Kentucky, but I do think my mother was pregnant at the time. I remember my mother retching and vomiting in the throat of the toilet and feeling the unrequited fear that there was something for which I was responsible.

"What's wrong, Mama?"

"Oh, Lynn, leave me alone!" she bleated.

I wanted my mother to be well. This went on for what seemed like a long time—every morning. I would hide in the closet and rock back and forth. "Leave me alone, Lynn. Leave me alone," I would repeat until the vomiting stopped. I had hated her, and now she was sick.

I wondered if it was my persistent bedwetting that caused this illness in my mother. After all, this caused my mother to be angry and sometimes spank me. Even when the misunderstood vomiting stopped, the spankings and complaining continued. I considered it my family chore to accept this discipline, because I had been the cause of her illness, and I was afraid she would get sick again.

After a few days of being away, my mother rushed in with a squalling infant wrapped in a blue blanket. I followed her to the room that had for many months housed an empty crib and changing table. She removed a cloth diaper and there was the naked baby.

"See, Lynn," she casually pointed out, "that's his penis."

It did not impress me, though it was a peculiarity. When the penis suddenly went up and he peed in my face. I took a more personal note and ran from my room to my dolls, where each doll received unrivaled love. I wanted to feel loved and safe. I would take all of them to bed with me and make sure they were tucked in and comfortable. They were very real babies to me, and I had an attachment to them that was as authentic as my attachment to any member of my family. My older sister and I often played with our shared children together.

I think the imaginary friends my sister creatively invented tell a harsh story about the unspoken difficulties of the abrupt change in our young lives. My sister was four years older than I, and looked after me in a way only an older sister, aware of the problems in the household, can. We had five friends: Eebie, Iibie, Oobie, Mary Beth, and Miss Eyebrow. Miss Eyebrow was our enemy, a taunting telephone operator who would not let us talk to our beloved friends. It is of interest that my mother had thick, thick dark eyebrows.

"May I speak to Eebie, please?" I would plead.

"Of course not," snapped Miss Eyebrow, "you did not eat all your oatmeal today." I would hang up the phone and sit in my rocker for a while. When I had my courage again, I would pick up the toy phone once again.

"Is Mary Beth home?

"No. She's dead."

This would start a torrent of tears, and Mother would send us to our room. Is Dad ever coming home I would ask myself, as I lay thinking of the friends I had left behind when we moved. Mary Beth and I had played together in a plastic pool. No, I have lost all my friends and my dad because I have been very, very bad. Mary Beth was the only "real" friend I could remember. Yet, I mourned over all the gone and unreachable past.

Shortly after my brother was born, things changed drastically. It was at this time that my mother's brutality became truly apparent. It was a change in venue. My mother went to work in my grandparents' business. My grandparents were successful merchants. When I was old enough to understand, I saw that all my mother's life she sought their approval. My grandfather was a strong figure in the life of my mother and us, his grandchildren. He supplied us with an allowance each week and without his position as the patriarch of our family, our lives would have been wretched.. He was a man of even temperament, always encouraging us to read and succeed in our education.

He, of course, had some aspects of his personality that were hurtful, but not intentionally so. My nickname was "Numbskull." This, I think, was because I was often daydreaming, and did not seem present. His desire was, I think, to pull me out of my own world, if he even knew I had my own world. Until I was much older, I did not understand that my life was full of violence and abuse.

My grandmother was a snobbish shrew whose scowling, critical dominance was probably the source of my mother's dissatisfaction with her own life and disapproval of her children. We were, as Mother's children, the representatives of her worth as a daughter. We were expected to be members of the upper echelon of our community, without flaw, to be seen with the right people, and to be perfectly groomed and dressed. My mother allowed her mother's intolerance to be like barbells resting on our shoulders.

My grandmother saw my emotional struggles as a lack of intelligence. I would have times when I could not respond. I could not even fully be aware of what in my intangible environment actually existed. Neither could I communicate to others, or understand what people were trying to communicate to me. There seemed to be an absence of thought. I was on my own island, waiting in silence to return from my static state to the place where others seemed to thrive. In school, my teacher's words would sometimes sound as if they were very distant, and I was an observer from miles away.

One evening, for example, I was spending the night with my grandmother. Her nickname for me was "Penny." She asked me to hand her an ashtray off the windowsill. For some reason, I could not understand what she was asking me to do. I felt stuck in time. I stood there standing, not responding.

"Penny," she said, frustrated, "sometimes I think you are not very bright."

"What?" I answered, my mind away from her, away from the grey carpet and the ashtray and the windowsill. I don't remember what was said or done or present that made me want to escape.

"You know, smart."

I must have been there, somewhere, because the words ring clearly, even today. It was one of many reactions I developed as I tried to fit in, to be what people wanted me to be. To have the friends my mother wanted me to have.

To look the way that everyone else seemed to look. The right clothes. The right shoes.

The new venue that brought on the era of physical abuse in my life was a house, purchased by my grandparents, for my mother and us children. It was an older brick home, painted white on Cherry Street, one block from Main Street.. There were four large bedrooms, which, instead of providing us with privacy, became cells of hell.

The night before our move from the apartment building where we had resided, my mother and grandparents took us to view our new home. It was furnished with antique furniture, hardwood floors, and flowered wallpaper. When my mother switched on the overhead light in my room, dozens of huge black bugs scurried under the wooden floorboards. This was the first horror I experienced in this cold house. I stood frozen. Then started crying.

"They are just water bugs,'" my mother said in an impatient tone.

I was grossly afraid of these black vermin. What if I was to step on one in the night? Or, worse, what if one got in bed with me? The fear was imprinted that winter when a matronly woman was caring for us while Mother and my grandmother were in New York on a buying trip for the store. We children were at the kitchen table waiting for a piece of cake. This was something Mother never made except on our birthday.

Across the floor ran one of those vermin, as big as a Buick. It ran under the floorboard, and the sitter was not going to let it get away. She ran after it with a table knife, and scooped it out. With her black oxfords, she stomped on the creature. Immediately poured out a white gruel.

"I've got to forget this," I said to myself. "I cannot let myself remember what that stuff looks like." However, no matter how hard I tried to forget, the image would haunt me with no known trigger. I would be ready to cross a street on my way walking to school, and the grueling image would spontaneously appear. The more I tried to get it out of my mind, the more often the image would appear.

"No, no, no," I would say to myself, "I will not remember!" But, of course, this approach just made the image indelible.

The night I first met my insect companions, I looked around at the yellow and white wall paper and white wainscoting. Looking back, it was quite tastefully decorated, but I had been promised a pink room. Between the water bugs and the disappointment of the color of my room, I stood unable to show any sort of enthusiastic comment about something which should have been a delightful moment.

"It's pretty," I finally was able to speak.

Of course, some disappointment and fear is inevitable in a child's life. But, when the fear becomes terror, and the disappointment becomes brutality, it is inevitable that scars are left, often handed down from generation to generation. I do not remember exactly when the unpredictable beatings began. My first memory of physical abuse occurred just after we moved into our own home.

One afternoon I came home from school, bouncing with joy from getting to tell a "story" in our third grade reading class. Everyone had laughed at my imaginative characterizations. I could not wait to tell Mother.

"Mother, guess what?" I greeted her.

Her eyes were immediately riveted at my feet. The detailed memory of what followed rings like the tintinnabulation of the bells in Poe's poem in my deepest heart of hearts. My mother's thick dark eyebrows came together in the formation of a centipede. I did not know yet what I had done, what was the encroachment on the ever changing rules that had bestowed upon me guilt.

"Did you let your grandmother see you like that?"

I had no idea of what she was talking.

Well? Did you go by the store?"

"Your sock is scrunched down in your shoe! You are a disgrace."

With that she grabbed me by the hair on the right side of my face. She dragged me to the yellow room where I at least found solitude with my dolls. The room with water bugs at night. She threw me on the floor and started kicking me in the belly. Worse, she started abusing me verbally.

"You are a nothing and a nobody! You always have been, and you always will be! No one likes you! You have no friends! You go around looking like a forsaken child, which you are!"

I lay on the floor long after she left and the beating was over. I touched my hair, and it came out in my hand. My sister and brother came home, and I lay there. Mother walked by the room, and peered in. As though surprised, she asked, "What's wrong with you?" It was as though she had no recollection of what had just transpired.

I remember being baffled, afraid, and very, very sad. I wondered if my dad was there, if this would have happened. I had many, many daydreams about saving my parents' marriage. In my dreams, I was either I was dying and they came together again on my deathbed, or I would do something outstandingly courageous, and they would come together out of pride in me.

It was Helen who kept me from sulking at home, lost in the world of abuse. After we moved into our house and Mother started working in the store, she employed "help." Help was considered an African American woman who was a domestic worker. Helen, our help, would not let me sit lazily watching cartoons on Saturday morning. She had me helping with the housework before I went to play with my friends.

"When I was your age, my mother had me doing all the housework while she worked for you white folks. Here. Sprinkle these clothes and roll them in a ball. While they is getting wet all over, do another chore. You start on the dustin', and I'll run the cleaner."

Helen taught me a lot about taking care of myself, and I loved her. Though I could not accept her Pentecostal beliefs, I listened to her when she talked about God. I was quite religious, even as a small child.

I read the Bible every night, though no one else in the house did. I believed Jesus wanted me to turn the other cheek, literally, and not rebel against the physical and emotional abuse my mother dished upon me.

Spirituality became my quest. Helen and I would dispute whether women should cut their hair. But, underneath—underneath the oppression that both of us experienced in our own ways—was the belief, that in the end, Good won.

We cleaned that house to Mother's specifications, which was not easy. Everything had a place. The items, in their place, were in the same place from the time we moved in the house until I graduated from high school and left home.

Mother had her rituals and her schedule. We ate our noon dinner on Saturday at 12:00PM, precisely. During the week Mother had supper ready at 5:30 PM, precisely. I remember being late once because I was having trouble with my bicycle, and Mother hit me over and over my body with a yardstick. I stood there without crying, thinking I deserved it because I WAS late. I lowered my head and let her hit me.

I was not allowed to turn on my light in my bedroom at night. We were required to sleep with our doors open. Bedtime was nine o'clock with no exceptions. There was to be no nagging to finish watching a TV program, or pleading to watch a special program.

During the time of all the physical abuse, I developed a fear of vampires. I had seen vampire movies on Saturday afternoon at the local theatre. It became an obsession. I bought a crucifix, complete with the bloody hands, feet, side, and forehead of Jesus. I had to hide it from Mother, for we were Methodists, and this was looked upon as a Roman Catholic relic. I slept for years with that crucifix on my chest. If I slept. Often, I would lie awake at night until the sun rose and pray, "Increase my faith, God. Increase my faith."

The crucifix was one item I secretly turned to for solace. Another was one whose intrigue I also hid from my mother, because we were not allowed to touch "her things." In the living room, which we were not allowed to live in, was a glass bowl with hand blown glass balls of different colors. My fascination was with the blue ball. I would, when Mother was not there, look into the ball and see all the distorted shapes. The world was transformed. The blue glass blown shapely showed a magical world, where there was Santa Claus, the tooth fairy, fairy tales that always had a happy ending. Unfortunately, there were all the hateful things that had been said to me and that I repeated to myself. It is part of all our minds. It is the world of magic that makes us hate and have delusional thoughts about the world. It is, in fact, the world of delusion, that must be shattered if the true nature of the world is to be seen—the world of natural phenomena, ever unfolding. Both worlds are actually reality. One is a matter of perception; one we only see in part, the objective experience.

Mother had her things, her life, and her routines. If something did not fit "in," it shattered her own feeling of security and happiness. Christmas was always a time of ritual and routine. Mother, at this time of year like some many people, wanted the world to be magical. We had a ritual we went through every year. We put on new pajamas and Mother read us Christmas stories. The same Christmas stories each year. We were showered with gifts when little affection was shown the rest of the year.

One Christmas Eve my sister, who being four years older than I, said the unthinkable. She said to Mother, "I am too old to hear these stories."

"What? You have ruined my Christmas! You don't give a damn about me! I have gotten you all these gifts, and this is the thanks I get? You selfish, mealy mouthed nothing!" Mother screamed.

It was a cold night, and the ground was frozen. "Here," she said, "here's your Christmas! Now open them!" With that she started throwing our presents out the back door onto the ground.

Not saying a word, not even to each other, we went outside this frigid Christmas Eve. Sitting on the hard, frozen ground, we began opening our gifts. Here was a precious new doll. Here was a chemistry set. Here was an elaborated round jigsaw puzzle. These gifts, which would have brought pleasure for months, or even years, were objects. Objects thrown at us by a deranged mother.

Mother disappeared into her room. Silently, with sadness and fear, we took our gifts to our rooms. Under my sheets and covers, I noticed a gentle snow outside my window, peacefully and quietly falling on the ground. All was calm. I comforted my new doll. It was not her fault. I told her I loved her, and cradled her in my arms. All was bright.

Although it was undeserved, we children kept silent about what when on in our home. The closest I came to revealing the violence was after school one afternoon when I went by to see my grandfather. I lay under a rack of dresses and ran my hands against the different textures. After about an hour, my grandfather asked, "Why don't you go home, Lynn?"

"Because I am afraid Mother will spank me," I replied.

My grandfather went to the phone and had a lengthy conversation with my mother. He came back and looked at me kindly. "It's okay. You can go home now."

I went home fearfully, for I did not know how Mother would respond. With great trepidation I walked into the house.

"I don't know why you said that to him," was all she said. The day went on, and it wasn't too much longer that the beatings continued.

The last beating I remember was a pivotal point in my life. I can't even remember why she was kicking me with those little pointed shoes of hers. But, I remember well the words.

"You are just like a little dog! You kick the dog and it comes back for more!"

What? Like a dog? The main reason I had not discussed the abuse with anyone was not fear for me, but fear for her. I feared if we were taken away from her it would destroy her. I would rather be kicked and abused than experience the demise of this woman, who lived her life through her children. I could not believe this attack. I had felt that I was doing the right thing, turning the other cheek. No more. No more would I live for this woman.

For several days I did not speak while in the house. I would go to meals and refuse to answer questions directed at me. Absolute silence. No tears. No rebuttal. Silence. Unfortunately, for a while it affected my life outside the home in the form of rebellion against all authority. I would talk out in class. I even cut a class with the student who was my best friend at the time—unheard of in the "advanced" class.

This went on for about six months. I remember being called to the principal's office the day we cut class. We had been turned in. I was sitting in French class and the teacher walked in front of me with a note asking her to send Lynn Campbell and Linda Hurtz to his office at 1:45 PM. She said to me so that no one else could hear, "Why don't you be good like your grandmother and your mother want you to be?"

Linda and I looked at each other with a look that said, "Oh my God! What have we done?"

This ended our phase of rebellion. Linda and I stopped conniving to cause trouble in classes. But, there was clearly a seed of anger inside me that had roots in my heart. I felt it sneaking to the surface at times when persons, especially persons in authority, showed any kind of weakness. I would take advantage of it.

There was poor Mr. Davis, a new young teacher who attempted to teach our Chemistry class. He was a short man with a crew cut, buck teeth, a huge dimple in his chin, and a high squeaky voice. The man did not stand a chance. It was not only I who disparaged his attempts to teach, but almost all of us. I, I think, was one of the worst. My first report card had an "A" in the subject matter and a "D" in conduct. I had walked across lab tables, without compunction had a soft drink and snack in class, and was totally out of control. Oddly, my mother's only response to my first grade report was, "How can you make a "D" in conduct and an "A" in the subject matter?"

One night at church I had an experience that redirected my anger and resentment. We were having a special service, and I was there without my family. We were singing the hymn "Blessed Assurance, Jesus is mine." I felt the same feeling I had felt at summer camp as we sat among trees, and moss, various ferns, and springs. A feeling would pierce me that was at once gave an awareness of peace and an awareness of who I really was. Summer camp was always a rich experience for me. There was no caste system; I was accepted and won badges and honors. The same god I experienced in the hills beyond the town, in the shimmering of the leaves of the silver maple, in the forsythia in bloom in our side yard, that God was the God I felt now in this group of people I often considered stiff and stuffy. I felt a need to go to the altar and ask God to forgive me for the hatred I had felt for my mother.

There was also a determination to live apart from the desires my mother had for me and live my own life. I changed that night. The friends with whom my mother wanted me to find acceptance were not the friends I wanted. They would allow me on the outskirts of the group, but not as a true member of the inner core. At the country club in the summer where we swam, I would often stay in the same area as these girls, though not really included with them, in order to avoid disapproval when I returned home with my mother.

With my new friends I wanted to say, "Wow! You like me!" although this probably would not have understood by them. We laughed. We giggled. We gossiped. We were teenagers. For me, it was delightful in high school at this time.

I developed into an unbridled extrovert. Or, so I let my friends and others see. Most of the time I was witty and sharp, but there were the deep dull times which I now recognize as depression. . I also had enormous expectations. I thought that once away from Mother, when I could make my own choices and live my own life, it would be easy. Life would not be so hard. I had no conception of what would be required to make that happen.

High school would end, and my friends would go to college or work. We would no longer be "the group." At my graduation I could hardly keep from weeping. Something told me the unfolding would be both a new freedom, but, also a lack of protection. The protection of what is familiar.

It was always expected that I would go on to higher education, and so I did. I was not goal oriented. I had no idea what to expect. I was going to University of Louisville and had never even visited it. I did not have the social skills to set limits in a relationship with men. I had only dated a little. I was a seventeen-year-old child. This was an ominous combination.

The summer before I went to college I worked in a home for children run by the Methodist Church. I spent many hours in my bed sleeping. I was deeply, deeply, depressed. Finally, I went home for a few weeks to gather the things I would need for school.

Johnny Appleseed

my father,
my Johnny Appleseed,
the lawyer, actually,
plants tulips and jonquil bulbs
by the hundreds
up the white and grey graveled drive
through the wooded area
where owls bleak at night
and raccoons scavenge
through the rubble

and Nature
is undisturbed

there are dozens
of young pines
and old oaks

and there is a beech tree
near the lake

with a used tire
for the young folks
to swing and squeal
with delight

the tall green grass
and the brown-green water
hide the frogs
and the bass and blue gill

the men
with tired souls
fish
and the women
with ancient wisdom
talk in the plentiful shade

Chapter Three

Johnny Appleseed

"Divorce" was not a term used inside or outside our home. It was not acceptable at this period in our country's history, much less in the strictly hidden private lives of our community. We were taught to use the word "separated." I was not clear whether, in fact, my parents were divorced.

When I was in the fourth grade I was determined to find out the truth on this matter. We were assigned to write an autobiography of one page for class, which for most was a listing of activities and organizations. Instruction was not given to include our undoubtedly painful inner life, and certainly we were not explicitly instructed to include the secrets of families, which actually told the most significant influences of our lives as small children.

After I wrote about my brother, my sister and the Brownie Scouts, I included that when I was four years old my parents divorced. I remember distinctly that I went to Mother as she was fixing supper.

"Mother," I asked, "can I read you my autobiography?"

"Yes. Go ahead," she answered as she was mixing something on the stove.

I remember well that she was pulling something out of the oven as I read the part about my parents divorcing. Her face, already scrunched from the heat of the oven, turned towards me.

"Oh," she bellowed, "do you have to put THAT in there?"

There was no denial of the truth of the statement. "Just put in there we moved here," she commanded in a more calm voice. I knew. It hurt. It would be more difficult to get my family together again. The truth is, we rarely saw Dad. Rarely were we even allowed to call him. On Christmas he brought lavish gifts, and we visited him for a week or two in the summer. When we did visit Dad in the summer, he did everything he could to make it a very special time. Dad always wanted to show us "the good life." We went to the movies, to the zoo in Cincinnati, to amusement parks, and we visited with our cousins—children of Dad's three brothers.

At my cousins' home in Lexington there was laughter, running, and hiding. Up and down stairs we went. We even slept in the bed with other children, if we stayed the night. My grandmother Campbell, who also lived in Lexington was a matronly lady. She always served mounds of country food, and we were allowed to have seconds . . . or even thirds, something Mother never allowed. I do not know if this was because of financial strain in Mother's life, or what else could have been the motivation. I know that when I heard about children going to bed hungry at night, I thought of my own growling stomach. I envied the life of my cousins.

Once, on one of our trips, with this man of manipulative charm, he pulled up in a red Oldsmobile convertible, top down. Mother was aghast.

"You're driving my children in THAT?"

"Oh, now, Pat, you know I'll drive safely."

"They could be killed!"

"Okay, okay, I'll drive with the top up," he offered as a concession.

"If I find out . . ." she threatened, her voice trailing off."

As soon as we were "out of range" the top went down. We raced down curvy country roads, and when we reached the parkway, we were sailing. All of us were squealing with delight, and I, normally afraid of anything that spelled danger, loved the feeling of "sneaking behind my mother's back."

It wasn't long, though, before the blue lights flashed. There was the state police. Dad instructed the three of us, "Don't you all say a word! Let me do the talking."

"Hello, Officer," he greeted the law enforcement officer, with his license, registration, and insurance papers.

"You were goin' pretty fast there, Sir."

"I am sorry, Officer, I was on a Sunday drive with my children. I wasn't paying attention. I'll slow down. I am an attorney in Louisville. I appreciate the Law."

"Well, try to keep your foot a little softer on the accelerator, Sir."

"Yes, Officer, of course. I appreciate it.'

"You have a good Sunday drive and drive safely."

"Yes, Sir."

As soon as the officer was gone and we were on the road again, Dad gave us our orders. "You are not to tell Pat about this or about having the top down, you understand?"

"Okay, Daddy," we chimed with glee. I felt I had a delicious secret. I craved my Dad's trust.

Drinking was also a part of Dad's life that we just accepted as normal. Until I was much older, I accepted the fact he always did something people who had fun did. They had a Bloody Mary in the morning. They sat in front a TV with a beer and Spanish peanuts. At night they had one last drink to put them to sleep. The fact that he constantly had a drink in his hand was something people who were fun loving and had a good sense of humor did. I don't think I ever saw my father sober.

He managed to function well in his constant state of inebriation. I had heard of alcoholics, but I thought they were drunks on the street—people who slurred their speech and couldn't walk straight. My father's position as an attorney with his own practice enabled his constant drinking. He always kept a variety of supplies in a small refrigerator and oak cabinet within arm's length of the swivel chair at his desk. Many of his buddies drank, and he almost daily met them at their favorite bar and restaurant before "calling it a day." We sometimes were taken to meet this rowdy bunch at one of these gatherings to be displayed like trophies from the days before he found freedom from our mother. Not until I was much older, did I consider the stress my mother was under, raising three children alone.

My father was from a working class family. He wanted us to see what it was like to be free from financial struggles. This was just one of the "finer" things we were taught. We ordered prime rib "medium rare." We were to leave big tips and make a show of it. "Here, Hon," he would say to a female server, "buy yourself a new pair of shoes."

Perhaps the most damaging value he taught was freedom from responsible sexuality. He often stated, "You marry a virgin; you make love to a whore." In my young mind, wanting to be loved, I interpreted this as having sex outside of marriage is the way to get love. It affected me later, though I was not conscious of where my own value as a woman had originated. Some would see me as promiscuous; some would see me as an abused woman who had not yet found her worth. Nor did I learn to respect myself as a person first and as a woman second. My ideas of what I wanted out of life were mixed up, like a tattered skirt and a silk blouse. I wanted my father's approval.

To one of his barroom buddies he commented, "Look at the ass on that bitch."

"Go for it!" his drunken companion with a rough skinned flushed face guffawed, "I'll give you a hundred, if you've got the equipment to do it!"

The whole line of slap-you-on-the-back men laughed in a deep, gut-throated good-old-boy response. I was learning that the way to get approval from men was to become a sexual object. Dad bought Crème de Menthe and slid it towards me to sip. It tasted good, but made me feel like I wanted to crawl in a corner and sleep. I pretended to be enthralled with the party. This was it. This was the life I wanted. It made people laugh. This is what it meant to have a good time.

We went back to our home with Mother, and the memories faded. There was one long period of time when we did not see our dad. Questioning Mother hesitantly, we got no clear answer as to why Dad was not showing up at Christmas, or taking us on visits in the summer.

On a sunny June day Dad reappeared. We did not know it, but our bags had been packed. There was the usual expression of affection from our father. He was a very affectionate father when we were with him. Something was being said between Dad and Mother that made me feel restless and unwilling to hear what was being spoken.

"You haven't told them," my dad said abrasively to my mother.

"No. I thought it was your responsibility."

I dismissed it quickly and ran out to the car. I hated adult secrets. They usually meant serious trouble. This seemed bigger than the irritability that always seemed to exist between them. I did not want to hear it.

I was unusually quiet as we took our usual route to Louisville. Dad seemed preoccupied. Then he cracked through my daydreams of all of us living together as a family. I lost my imaginations of a father that would see that we could have a second helping of mashed potatoes. That he would tuck me safely in bed at night. That the horrid beatings would stop.

"I have to tell you three children something. You have a new stepmother and a baby brother."

None of the three of us had discussed with each other the hope that our family would be together again. My brother had not even lived with my father. My sister seemed so much wiser than I. It like I was dealing with it alone. I started crying.

"Damn it. I knew it would upset you," he said as though exasperated. He added, "Come on now. I still love you children."

After a while I stopped crying. The lush green trees on either side of the road stood as strong as ever. The sky had wisps of clouds lazily moving like protective ghosts to show me that things were actually the same. The truth of the yellow light in the sky was the truth of an illusion that had been destroyed, of an imagined life that, in fact, never existed. And would never exist.

After a quiet ride we pulled into the drive. My eyes immediately went to the lake with brown-green water and a dock with a metal row boat. There were pastel wildflowers where the grass had not been cut. Two German Shepherds ran to greet their master.

Our new stepmother greeted us at the door. I took my father's hand and smiled a half smile that said, "I am not sure about you."

As it turned out my stepmother was a middle school teacher, and very adept at dealing with children. We heard a fussing and noisy crash and she brought out a darling boy. I loved him immediately. He was like one of my dolls—only alive. It did not take long to see we would be treated as out stepmother's own children. Our days were filled with shopping, swimming, and household chores. I spent much time playing with this little one. I adored him.

I was trusted to cook the meat on the grill behind the house. I was overtly thrilled that my stepmother was willing to teach us the life in a cohesive family. Even my Mother's son, who was about five, had chores that he willingly did. He, too, seemed content to be here, though I did not talk to him about how he felt.

My sister had a question for my stepmother. "Who is prettier, me or Lynn?"

With what I think was wisdom she answered, "Well, I think maybe Lynn is prettier, but you are more attractive."

Every day before Dad left for work he pulled us aside. "Now, you three help out with the work. Okay?"

This, in all honesty, hurt my feelings. I was trying to help. I was doing what was asked. I was learning to love my baby brother. How could he not see that?

My greatest joy was playing with the baby. I thought he was so funny. I loved to make him laugh. I wanted a baby of my own.

We were not allowed to do chores at home, at least when Mother was there. We were "in the way." Once after being at summer camp where we, under supervision, cooked and cleaned up afterwards over an open fire, I took it upon myself to do the dishes for my mother.

"What are you doing?" She asked, annoyed.

"I am doing the dishes for you."

"Just get out of the kitchen. I'd rather do it myself. You aren't supposed to clean a cast iron skillet that way anyway," she snapped, as I scrubbed on the black pan.

Our visit with Dad and our new stepmother was delightful to me. Our cousins came! There were children running in and out of the house, constantly being reminded to keep the door closed.

I returned home wanting to share my excitement. I was full of stories of words I had taught the littlest brother, and how I had been able to watch him for short periods of time.

However, Mother shortly put an end to the stories. When my brother and I were sent to our grandparents' house for a Sunday afternoon visit. Mother soon squelched my enthusiasm by admonishing, "And, don't fill your grand-mother's ears with all those stories about that baby, either."

Even my joy was turned into something for which I should feel shame. I did not grasp the dissension between two families I still thought of as one.

Not of all of Dad's personality fostered love, as became more and more apparent as I grew older. I saw the difficulties my mother and his second wife experienced. The idealized image of my father was like any of the distorted images I viewed in that magical blue glass ball.

I grew to understand my father as I grew older, and I loved him even though his sexual innuendos, his heavy drinking and smoking, and that cruel streak became rebarbative. He was an ex-Marine in World War II. This un-doubtedly affected his character. He fought in the Philippines, seeing the worst of gruesome death and destruction. As a radio operator he had much added responsibility. He was allowed to carry a small book with him; he carried a dictionary. Definitely an intelligent man, he got his GED when he returned home, and eventually finished law school, hoping to be an FBI agent. Unfortunately, a back injury prevented him from achieving that goal. In his era, FBI agents had to be attorneys. At least had a career on which he could follow, and he did so successfully

For three years before his death, I called him every morning at 11:00 to check in on him. He was suffering and COPD, and eventually died in his late 60's of lung cancer.

My mother, too, became more of a person to pity than a witch I feared. She was a lonely woman—living her life through her children. Our failures—no matter how small—were her failures. When she called me a "nothing," I believe she was talking of how she felt about herself. Forgiveness has been very difficult. I finally reached an understanding that forgiveness was about me. About letting go—not as important for her as for me. Holding on to hatred meant hating myself as well. I had to accept that I have many of her characteristics. I was part of her, but she, also was and is part of me.

I had idolized my father. I remember when I saw the jagged crack in my father's character—his deep lack of sensitivity in his approach to others. I was deeply degraded and humiliated.

I was at the sensitive age of fifteen. My father and stepmother took my brother and me to Virginia Beach with his "other" family. Two-piece bathing suits had come in style. I had tried on bathing suit after bathing suit in my grandparent's store. With my small breasts the tops hung limp. Then my grandmother brought out this ugly red-orange one piece suit. She stuffed the top with falsies.

"That looks good," my mother directed her comment to my grandmother.

"Well, I think so," she replied. I had my bathing suit, which was nothing but an embarrassment to me.

At the beach I wore a hot sweat shirt over the hideous bathing suit. When the heat became unbearable, I slipped the sweat shirt off and ran for the water.

I heard my dad and stepmother talking. "Why would Pat let her go around looking like that?" my father asked.

My stepmother replied, "I can't imagine!"

Then we were walking from a restaurant in the town area, and we stopped in front of a pre-teen clothing store. "Here's where we are going to get you a new bathing suit," my stepmother said to me. I was delighted.

"And don't put any of those big things in it either!" my father spat out. I loathed myself at that point. I even, quite earnestly, wished I was dead. I saw through a crack in the wall a glimpse of the cruelty of which he was capable. I dismissed that thought, and only wished I were a different someone. Yet, the memory of that horrid bathing suit was put in a compartment in my mind. I was delighted to look like a normal teenager. I had a wonderful trip after that. Miracles happened. I even had a date with a young man who was quite polite and respectful. He was in the Navy, and he, too, just here for a short time. I met him on the beach and we talked of our home towns. We talked of trivia, which was like a soothing tonic to my soul, troubled as it was with the conflicts between myself and others, myself and a future that was so hidden it could not even say my name.

This was just the beginning of my realization that my father showed no inhibition in his comments or behavior or sensitivity to how they affected a person. I began to see him do this to others. I began to notice he gambled heavily. He had a bookie and ran a tab. He would bet on anything from tennis to horses. I heard him make racial slurs. Even at someone merely walking in front of the car at a crosswalk. People who had done nothing to him. Worst of all, I watched the harsh anger he expressed towards my stepmother for insignificant incidences. I developed a fear of his disapproval. Here was the father who held me in his lap. Here was the man who found me incapable and of deplorable demeanor.

"Why did you let a goddamn spoon get in the disposal?"

"Well, now, it was an accident."

He was a tall overpowering man who could look at you with absolute disgust. He was extremely impatient. As I grew older, I became an object for his sexual comments.

Once I asked for a swab for my ear after swimming. "What are you going to do with it, masturbate?" He asked. The older he got the cruder he became. I do believe all the alcohol had affected his brain. I saw less and less of the man I had idolized, and more and more of a cynical, sick, alcoholic.

As a young child I would not let myself see this. I saw his love of nature. I saw him plant tulips and jonquils by the hundreds. How could someone be so close to the essence of this colorful earth, something I myself revered, and be so insensitive to the people whose life came from the same source?

Yet, my stepmother was good for Dad. She expected him to take responsibility for her and his children. She made sure he was punctual for his appointments and was dressed handsomely. This did not stop his drinking or stops to his favorite bars after work or after a court date. My guess was she accepted the limits in her influence on his behavior.

She and Dad had another baby, a little girl who I also loved. I fed her and played with her. When I grew up, I wanted a little girl. I would give her dolls. I would give her the small wooden rocker that played "Rock-a-Bye Baby" when it moved that my grandmother had given me when I was three. We could dress the dolls in frilly little outfits and coo at them. We could push the dolls in strollers and pretend we were in the park.

Oddly, Dad was good with children. He would make them laugh and introduce them to new foods that most children would never touch. Small children were exempt from his cruel streak. Once adulthood came close though . ..

Around the time my mental illness became apparent, Dad and my stepmother divorced. It was quite a sad time in all our lives, even Dad's, though he tried to make a joke out of it. He lost everything. The land. His lake. He had been having an affair for some time. "A mighty expensive piece of ass," he would say to his friends. They would shake their heads and howl. But, I would see him sitting in the dark with a cigarette glowing as he began the process of moving out of a home no longer his. I saw a pain in him that was a new side to him of, which I was becoming aware. His children, his wife—they were gone also. Maybe, he saw what he had brought on himself. Maybe it wasn't as hilarious as he made his "buddies" believe.

It was confusing for me, his sexual activity. It seemed he loved his family, but for some reason would risk everything for "a piece of ass." It made me wonder if it was better to be the one stuck with the diapers and the housekeeping, or the one who got taken to dinner and received flowers.

I stayed with him that summer before he bought more land and built his dream cabin in the woods. I know he was lonely after that, even though men came to fish in his lake and families came for picnics. His health was not good, and his life was basically over. He would sit quietly on his redwood deck. He did enjoy the woods and the animals he saw.

Unfortunately, at this time he also became more sexually abusive.

"You smell!" He said to me once. "Are you keeping that thing clean?"

As we both became older, his verbal abuse became overt sexual abuse. This was years later when I was an adult, but suffering greatly from severe mental illness. His drinking was out of control and so was he. As I stood in his rustic kitchen, he would approach me and I knew what was coming. He would grab one of my breasts in each hand clinching his teeth like he was petting a beloved pet.

My complicated mental illness had not yet improved to the realization that I did not have to be a victim. I allowed people to manipulate me and based my actions, not on mutual benefit, but on what I thought would win their approval. All too often, it was inappropriate and only brought on more pain and rejection.

He was so unabashedly shameless, that he would do this in front of other people, but would not do it in front of other family members. I suppose he suspected they would "not understand."

"I like Lynn's breasts better than her older sister's," he said once in front of a female guest who was staying the night. "They are more, I don't know, they are just . . ." He did not finish his explanation.

Finally, my best friend Lynda helped me realize what my father was doing to me. I don't know whether she had observed this, or I had simply told her about his disrespect.

"Don't you see this is sexual abuse?" She probed.

"I don't think he means anything by it. He is just showing affection."

"Well, why does he take the liberty to do this to you?"

"I guess he loves me."

"If I grabbed my son's penis, would you think I was being merely affectionate?"

I laughed hysterically at the visual image. But, I was there. Face-to-face with the stark realization of what was going on. It was sexual abuse. Very sly sexual abuse, masked by an amiable approach.

Shortly after this enlightening discussion, I was visiting my father in his house in the woods. One of his female companions and I were having a Thanksgiving meal together. He was fixing the meal primarily for me because my half-sister would not include me at her home. My illness, and consequently my poverty, was an annoyance and an embarrassment. This was the kind side of my father. The reason I can forgive him for the crude side of his character.

Unfortunately, his sickness came to play. I was standing in the kitchen and he walked up and grabbed my breasts.

"If you do that again, I'll walk out of this house and never come back," I said quietly, but firmly. He had a shocked look and walked away. Then he walked towards me again.

"I meant what I said." I could not believe these words were coming out of me.

But, never again did he touch me in such a manner. I do not know where the strength to set these boundaries originated. Even in that far away distant place where I went when caught in a corner, the fight was there. I simply had to break through the haze and speak. Courage is not the absence of fear; it is the strength to act in face of it.

I once discussed this with my older sister. She said, "Gosh, I don't know what I would have said if he had done that to me." I am assuming he would never have done that to another member of the family because there would have been an outrage. But, who would believe a certified crazy person? Or, so I thought. I learned something valuable, though. The only way to deal with the monster, Fear, is to face it squarely. Look at it in its many disguises, straight in its eyes, and know it for what it is.

What happened to my Johnny Appleseed? What happened to the affectionate father who would walk us around the lake and point out the names of blossoming trees? He was there. He was flawed, like all of us. The parts I loved, I still love.

My father died with all his children around him. He had once told me, "Don't think I don't see the way they treat you." His estate was left to me.

waiting

waiting
for the touch
the feeling of
in me
to wish
that not tomorrow
oh to soon
you hate the same
my womanhood
the fingernails
the softness
still waiting
for you
does sense
the same
in which
a woman's softness
senses

question
and desire

Chapter Four

Waiting

Going up the side stairs to the orange dorm with arms filled with a well-planned fashion statement of clothes, my mother and I silently made our way to the fourth floor where the exuberant freshmen would make a home in sets or two out of a concrete rectangle. I could barely fight back the tears. It surprised me. I had wanted to get away from her, yet I knew the small town in western Kentucky would never be my home again. My mother . . .this was the person, as difficult and cruel as she could be, would always see that I had clothes, a home, and food.

As it always had been, I could not express what I truly felt. I did not want her to comfort me, for I did not want to include the tender side of her for my appraisal. Yet, I wanted to hold her in my arms. I don't know whether it felt false, or if, because of her abuse, I could not acknowledge that there was, in fact, a bond of love, though it seemed irrational, existed between us. I would find it too confusing to view a sort of multiple-sided personality. It was easier to keep it simple. Love and hate were two extreme poles. Or, were they? Like desire that turns to aversion. Or, maybe things we love disappear, just like things we don't love. Perhaps I was seeing the impermanence of all things, whether we desire them or have aversion to them.

When I was a small child, I would hide in the house when I was sick. I could not tolerate the overly concerned face she would bear, or the pain she would show others about whatever illness I had. Often even when I would have

47

a raging fever. Or, a rash that meant I was sick. Whatever the symptom, I did not want to be found. Wherever I was, eventually, I would be missed; the hunt would begin, and I would be found. Being found would mean I would be taken to bed and the doctor would be called. In these days, if it was after office hours, the doctor would come to our home with his black bag.

I was terrified of doctors. I thought the doctor would tell me I was going to die. The obituaries Mother would read at the breakfast table aloud—the stories of people of all ages dying of cancer, the woman getting a bubble in some sort of tube in her blood vessels while being treated and dying—all these told me I, too, would die. By age four I knew all living things had no certainty. No security. This is why I read the Bible. If there was hope, it was in God.

At this moment of separation from my mother, I was grieving. Never again would things be as they were. What lay ahead? I thought of the collection of some twenty ceramic angels for which I had saved my allowance to buy, placed carefully on the mantel in my room. I thought of my globe with the light in it that made it shine blue-green on my oak desk in my bedroom. I thought of my blue glass ball that had been my escape. How could I escape this moment?

But, my mood changed swiftly as we entered the hallway lined with metal doors. This was the women's side of the dorm, and women were coming in and out of doors. Many had towels wrapped around there head as they came from the communal shower and bathroom. The floor was buzzing, full of laughter.

We found our way to or my assigned room. My roommate was not there, though her belongings were. There was extra-long bed to either side with a simple desk and chair at the end. A closet with sliding drawers, set of drawers with a mirror above it. Each room had a heating and cooling unit. That was it.

With little talk, my mother and I began hanging up my clothes, filling up the drawers, and making up the bed. Mother put up my shoes, a pair to go with every outfit, with toes pointed in the same direction and aligned perfectly.

Finally, we said goodbye, which was anticlimactic after the trek up the side stairs. By this time I was anxious to meet the bubbling women who were openly warm in greeting me, and showed they were eager to help me find my way through the difficulties of orientation, scheduling of classes, and registration. We freshmen were told there would be long, long lines and much frustration.

The money had been put in my checking account by my grandfather for expenses; all I had to do was write a check. There was anxiety; there was excitement. I wondered if the other freshmen felt the same as I.

I talked for a couple of hours with a student named Nickie. We shared that we both wrote poetry and exchanged some of our writing.

"Can you write as well when you are not down on the world," I inquired.

"Sometimes. Like when I really feel high, like when I've accomplished something. But, if I'm just bumming around, the stuff just won't come."

"I just write from my experience. I mean, how can you write a poem about sex if you haven't experienced it?"

"Well, you can write about it from your perspective."

"I don't know. I tend to write about what is going on in my life. I mean, unless it's a paper or assignment or something. Are you going to try to get in the creative writing class?"

"Not this semester. I am hoping my writing will improve with some of the English classes I am taking."

I met my roommate Jackie after our conversation. When I returned to our room she was there. She was somewhat reserved, but seemed very considerate.

"Where are you from?" I asked her.

"Connecticut."

"I am from a small town in western Kentucky. Mother has already said you can come home with me for Thanksgiving. What do you plan on studying?"

"I want to be a marine biologist. I am going to get the basic courses here."

"I want to study theatre arts and creative writing. They actually don't have a theatre arts major. I have to major in English with an emphasis in theatre arts. Also, tomorrow I hope to get permission from the instructor to take a creative writing course."

"Is Lynn your first name? I was told it was Elizabeth."

"Elizabeth is my first name, but I go by Lynn, my middle name. You are my roommate, so I'll call you 'Room'."

"I will call you Room 2."

"No. I don't like to be in second place. We will both be 'Room'."
We got into the heavy stuff. Both of us came from divorced parents, and we had been raised by our mothers. Neither of us knew people at the school except there was one guy, named Tom who came from the same town as I. We had

not associated with each other in high school, although he was a really nice, intelligent guy. My roommate had never been in Kentucky before.

I had not talked to my father since I got to school, so I gave him a call at his office. He was rather aloof, but said maybe one day we could get together for lunch. I tried to act like I was not disappointed.

"Dad! I am here," I had almost screamed.

"Good, Hon. We'll get together for lunch sometime."

Sometime, I thought. *I wonder when that will be*. But since a date was not set for lunch, I got off the phone and quickly switched gears with my roommate to obscure his disregard for me, his daughter.

I gathered Room's father had little interest in her life, either. In our conversations about our friends at home, or in what activities we had been involved, we scarcely talked about our fathers.

Then, out of the shelter of the night, as we were lying in bed, the big question was asked. I had not dated much in high school, and my group of friends and I never considered "going all the way." One of my friend's sister had become pregnant and dropped out of school. It was considered disgraceful to her family, Although her family was quite disturbed and angry at first, they offered love and protection to her baby, to her, and to the baby's father. The unwed couple married, and they were accepted in our Puritanical community once the whispers grew old. The big question stood with as much importance as the grades we made in school. I questioned Room, which was quite brazen of me.

"Room," I asked, "are you a virgin?"

"Yes," she said with shyness and something akin to embarrassment. "Are you?"

"Me, too. Let's make an agreement we share if that should change."

"I will promise if you will, too."

"Sure. You'll be the first to know. Well, the second."

We laughed. She then teased me. "Does it count if it is with a woman?"

I buried my head in my pillow and howled. "No, that doesn't count!"

"Well, first of all, we have to get a date!" The two of us laughed and talked, not worrying about it getting closer and closer to dawn. Then we drifted off to sleep. The promises of life as an adult was something of which we had dreamed, but, for me anyway, were as blank as a white canvas and as mysterious as an unopened book. Truly, we had begun a search. The very values we had clung to as children would be tested, changed, reversed, and changed again. My roommate had a certain sadness about her that made me wonder about the pain in her childhood. Although I carried a great heaviness, I thought mine was more hidden. Perhaps, not.

I embraced college life with fear, but at the same time with grandiose expectations. I had just assumed, for example, I would be welcomed into the creative writing class without any difficulty, but, the response would somehow be disappointing. I had to have the professor's permission to be in the class, so the next day I found my way to his office.

"Are you Dr. Weber?" I asked upon entering his office.

He leaned back, and I watched him remove a small cigar from his mouth. He looked at me as though he were summing me up and I stood there naked.

"What can I do for you?" He asked, without acknowledging my question.

"I wanted to get in your creative writing class. I brought you some of my poems and essays," I said as I offered them to him.

He took the writings, and leaned back in his chair, puffing once and a while on his cigarillo. He placed the papers upon his desk as though considering. I was not breathing. My self-confidence immediately plummeted to self-loathing. Why did I come in here with these papers my first semester? A girl from the country thinks she's great until she bombs out.

Then, as he twisted his moustache, he said, "You have some good images. I'll sign your advisor's slip." I didn't have one yet, but promised to come by as soon as I had seen my advisor.

I felt ecstatic and depressed. I had hoped for a more positive response, but I did get in the class. He told me there would be eight to twelve students in the class. I promised myself I would make him see that I had a great future as a writer.

The process of registration began the next day. I went to see my advisor. When she asked what my major was going to be, I told her I wanted to major in English with a specialization in Theatre Arts.

"Do you have any experience in acting?" She asked when I told her what my major would be.

"I had the lead role in our Senior Play."

"Have you had any *training*?" she persisted.

51

"Not really," I said, lowering my gaze.

"Well," she stated, "I strongly recommend you take Voice and Diction."

I agreed to do that, and would become aware of why she so insisted when I went to my first class. I thought little of it at the time.

There was a lot going on during the period of registration. One of them was a tea to select the ten best dressed women on the campus. I went in a cream colored, textured A-shaped dress with a large gold broach below my rolled neckline. We were greeted by the judges and talked briefly to them. Then it was announced. I was one of those selected. Wait until the people in my home town saw my picture plastered on the Society Page! It sent me into a high, and I was sailing as though running like a child through the meadows, flailing my arms at the sun. Surely, the angels were applauding. It never occurred to me that others saw my grandiosity as intrusive and offensive.

Finally, the first day of classes. My first reaction was that it was going to be so much easier than high school. My first class was not until ten in the morning. I could stay up late and work, as I liked to do. I placed out of several classes. It seemed so simple. Just do the work. Attendance was not mandatory in many of the classes. It all seemed like fun. I regret, looking back, I did look further into the future. *How, realistically, could I support myself once my education was completed?*

However, my first day in my Voice and Diction class, I was knocked down several notches, at least for a little while. Our instructor had us read a soliloquy from a play I cannot remember. After we read the piece, she would tell each student what areas in which they needed to work. This person needed to work on the "a" or a more distinct "t". I saw this as an opportunity to give expression to what I read. I read dramatically, but there was something that was making the other students whisper and chuckle.

"Where are you from?" She asked as though asking a honest question

"Muhlenberg County, KY."

"Well, I knew you were from somewhere out there!"

The class howled, but one student in a maxi dress with large bosoms and a large body came to my defense. "Don't dare change anything about her voice! She is adorable!"

I was humiliated. My first day in a drama class, and I was ridiculed. But, I tried not to show it. I laughed with everyone else. I was a wonderful actress at that point. I acted like I found this funny and enjoyed being adorable when, in fact, I was ashamed of my hometown, myself, my family, and, most of all, that I thought I could compete on a university level. I was dumb and stupid. I was dumb and stupid. The glass ball spoke the truth.

After class a tall blond male approached me—a member of our class. And he was good looking.

"Hi. Where are you headed?'"

"To my next class."

"Mind if I walk with you?" We walked a little further, and then he formally introduced himself. "As you heard in class, my name is Glenn."

"As you heard in class, my name is Lynn," I said, "and I'm from Muhlenberg County."

"Don't worry about it. You'll probably be the only one to ace the course." We walked by the next building without speaking. And then he picked up the conversation. "I'm in a play at a community theatre in town. I was wondering if you would like to go with me to the rehearsal tonight." I was excited to hear about "community theatres," but didn't want to display my ignorance. I answered, "Well, I live in the dorm, and I have to be back by eleven."

"Sure. Sounds great."

Glenn added in parting, "I'll pick you up at six. We'll get a bite to eat first, okay?"

"It's a date!"

He smiled, and I waved. Perhaps I wasn't like what I thought. I couldn't wait to tell Room about my first date. I went to French class upbeat, and ready, once again, to take on college life.

In my hometown I was unused to attention from boys. Most of my girlfriends had boyfriends for the purpose of the prom, dances, or other big events. Certain cliques dated certain circles of students. No male appeared to be interested in me. For this reason, I was astonished that on the first day of class, I had a date and he was a really cute guy. Wow! I came back to the dorm elated and talking so fast Room could hardly understand me.

"Slow down, Room," she said laughing.

"What do you think I should wear?"

"I think your pant suit."

"What will I do if he puts the moves on me?"

"Don't let him! Guess what?"

"What?"

"I have a date, too!"

"Tonight? Who with?"

"No, not tonight. Friday. With a football player."

"NO KIDDING!"

"No, I'm not kidding!"

"Where are you going?"

"We're going to dinner, then a movie."

We went on rattling about classes and guys. I started getting ready for my first date to the community theatre. I really did not know what to expect. My make-up, clothes, shoes and purse all coordinated, as was usual for me at this point in my life. I waited for the phone to ring from the lobby.

Finally, Glenn called, and I was so excited that I kept dropping things out of my purse as I was looking to be sure I had my lipstick. Eventually, I made it downstairs, and there was the darling Glenn. He was really clean-cut for what I had envisioned an actor to appear. He wore khaki pants and a pinstriped shirt. I doubted he had spent as much time on his appearance as I had on mine.

We went the theatre, which was downtown in a rather rundown building with obviously old curtains and dismal wooden walls. I sat in on a thick cushioned seat that sank deep towards the floor. It reminded me of the Palace Theater back home. Glenn introduced me to the cast and the director as they were going about, preparing for the rehearsal. I felt my stomach tighten with anticipation.

When the lights went down, a golden aura lit the setting. It was a rustic Western set with an appealing smoothness to it. Obviously, the set was carefully designed. I watched as the actors, in the later stages of preparation for their first performance, began to rehearse. Leo, the stage manager who was an actor of some notoriety in the area, invited me to the balcony to see how the stage lights were managed.

Leo showed me the levers that moved the lights up and down. Periodically, he left to coach his two brothers, who had roles in the play. We had moments to talk, and he asked me if I wanted to be the prop mistress. I felt a surge of adrenalin spreading from my stomach to my brain. He explained what I would have to do, and I agreed that I could do that with no difficulty. It was my introduction to the theatre. It was also my introduction to Leo.

In other arenas, my values and beliefs were being challenged. In my philosophy class I was beginning to see that my small town Christian beliefs were not the only way to look at the world. I read the introductory philosophers voraciously. I even was invited to read my first paper in class. The professor said it exemplified the way a paper should be written. My spirits were lifted higher and higher. I began to have a rather cavalier attitude towards life.

Room and I would joke. "Should I skip class to go shopping with one of my friends?"

"Well, of course, after all, we are going to die anyway." We would laugh, but I was taking this much further than my roommate. I was basing decisions on beliefs that would affect my life in ways that would last for almost a lifetime.

"Do we have a choice in what we do?" We would joke about this also.

"Hell, no!" We are products of our biology and circumstance. This attitude, though arguably true, is a very dangerous way to live one's life. It negates the necessity of taking responsible action.

I was in the mode of thrill seeking and having fun. I was amazed at how easy it was to make friends and get dates. I turned down many dates, which possibly could have led to meaningful relationships. I was attracted to the false glitter and glory of a life with experiences that the Buddha described as like "painted chariots" passing by. Painted gold, but only rotten wood beneath. I took my new position as prop mistress seriously, though. Every night Glenn picked me up. Glenn was a very gentle, ethical person. Too bad his friend Leo did not also have his values. Leo had quite a bit of acting talent, and was destined to be successful. He was red-headed and burly, and had a confidence that appealed to me. Unfortunately, I was more interested in charm and prestige at this point in my life than in character.

Leo and I began meeting in the balcony when we both had free moments. We began teasing and telling stories that were both fantasy and fact, leading each other to the end of the tale, then dropping casually the truth of the matter.

"My dog could tell who was a virgin or not."

"How?" Leo asked, playing along.

"By the way they bit you when you held out your hand."

"Yeah, how?"

"Like this," I teased, biting at his arm.

This was enough to invite him to grab my head and begin kissing me. I felt warm and aroused. But, I had to leave to get the props ready for the next scene.

Our relationship was moving quickly beyond playful bantering. I started slipping up to the balcony at every chance, and we engaged in heavy petting and overt sexual activity. I know Glenn found out at some point, although I cannot remember when.

Fall was leading into winter, the season of death, I had always thought. The play opened, and Leo and I continued our play. I had a lot to learn about relationships between men and women. My dad's message seemed to be that it was desirable to be "a piece of ass." I cannot remember where or what led up to the actual act. I remember being somewhere in bed with Leo, and we did it. We had sex. Or, more descriptively, he performed sex. There was little foreplay. There was little affection. There was lust. It was more like a dog hunching a bitch. I was disappointed in the experience.

I came back to the dorm and Room and I were lying in the bed talking. "Room," I whispered , "I'm not a virgin anymore."

"What? You and Leo? Did you have an orgasm?"

"What's an orgasm?" I asked innocently.

"*What's an orgasm?* Woman! I am going to have to get you some books!

"I guess we can safely say I didn't have one."

With that we both laughed hysterically, and I started filling her in on the details. At the time, I did not see this was a pivotal point in my life. I did not see that the "fun" was a dangerous sword, slashing through everything that had existed and pointing to a new direction my life would take.

Following the opening night of the play was the closing night of our relationship. It was Saturday going into Sunday, and we went to the usual cast party waiting for the excellent reviews the play received. Leo and I left together. As we *lay* in bed Sunday morning, Leo suddenly popped out of bed and said, "I am going to miss Mass! We have to go! And this stuff has to stop! I could be arrested for statutory rape!"

"What are you talking about? You are going to miss Mass? You are going to Mass?"

He apparently didn't see the irony I saw in this situation, *He's in bed with a seventeen-year-old girl who until now was a virgin, and he is afraid of missing Mass? And now, now he is going to end it??* I couldn't believe what was happening to me! I don't know what I thought would be the outcome of our relationship, but I didn't expect this! Even the girl who got pregnant in my hometown got married! To think he did not love me was not comprehensible.

Interestingly, I thought I was both better, and at the same time less adequate than my fellow students.. I did ace that Voice and Diction course, but I did get a "C" on my English term paper. I thought Leo was unreachable to most women in my peer group, but I was in denial that our affair was over. I continued on a roller coaster of moods that went to the heights and then would take my breath as it went on its course down the narrow rails.

In truth, I envied Room. She did not have the flighty slips in and out of elations and despair. She had to work harder at what she achieved, but she was willing to do that. She fought each step with a determination that would ensure she reached a tangible, realistic goal.

Room would ask about Leo and me. "Did he call?"

"Not yet."

He had left the city. I do not remember where. I would write him letters that were never answered. Something started happening after my first rejection by a male who used me and then tossed me aside. Winter had come. The last leaf had found its way to the ground. As I walked back to the dorm in the late afternoons, the cold made me hunch my shoulders and lower my head. Voices started coming from the shrubs as the wind rustled through.

"Mary, Mary, are you there? Look at all the eyes who stare. You're a whore with nothing left to share."

I kept thinking that if I was going to die, it might as well be now. Thoughts of suicide recurred, especially at night. I thought leaving home meant getting away from pain, getting away from home, having my own life, making my own decisions. Instead, I was more miserable than I had ever been. I lay on the bed contemplating my decision. Leo would show no remorse. I would be dead eventually, anyway. Why not now? There would be no more pain. There would be no more voices. Sure, some people would be shocked, maybe grieve. But, soon their lives would go on. I would just be a memory. I was in my own glass ball.

I started taking the bottle of aspirin I had bought for the purpose. I washed down the bitter taste with a Coke. I lay there thinking that soon I would go to sleep and die.

But, I did not die. I began retching. I was vomiting into a trash can and was sicker than I had ever been in my life. I pictured myself retching up all the deceit, the hidden agendas, the manipulations. It was all coming up.

"What is wrong?" I heard my roommate demanding. *"Have you been drinking?"*

"What is this?" She saw the empty bottle of aspirin on my bed. *"You overdosed!"*

At the time I did not understand her anger. I did not see I had opted out, and now she had to deal with the mess. All I knew was I was sick. Very sick. She called her sorority big sister who lived in the dorm, and she came to see what they should do. They went to the lobby and got milk and told me to drink it. The milk felt good on my stomach. I was happy to drink it. My ears were ringing terribly. It was deafening, and I could barely make out their words. In retrospect, it was probably the vomiting that saved me.

I wish now I could make amends with these people. I wish I could say I was sorry to Glenn, Room, and others. But, they have disappeared out of my life.

Dr. Ehrler's Office

twelve stories
above the city
in my psychiatrists office
I looked through

a window

rock-a-bye bus
to the rhythm
of old ghosts

rock-a-bye bus
to the rhythm
of old songs

pieces of musical literature

pieces of old songs

an airy sonata
to a select audience

Chapter Five

Dr. Ehrler's Office

The day after my overdose I awakened with my ears still ringing. My stomach burned. I felt like I HAD died and awakened in hell. My roommate heard me stirring and asked how I was doing. I told her, "Like hell."

"You are going to have to see someone," she informed me, "a psychiatrist."

"Okay."

"If you don't call someone today, I am going to the dorm director."

"I will."

I got the yellow pages and looked in "physicians" for psychiatrists. Here was one Fourth Street. That was on a direct bus route. I would go see him. I told my roommate I would see a Dr. Ehrler. I would take a shower and take a bus. I had no idea what to expect. We did not even have a psychiatrist in our hometown.

I showered and dressed, though I did not give a damn what I looked like. I just did not want to smell like vomit. I brushed my teeth, put on make-up, went ahead and fixed myself up. I decided it was best to look like I gave a damn about myself.

I did not make an appointment. I had no idea what the protocol was. I assumed if I said it was an emergency, he would see me.

"I'm catching the next bus," I told my roommate. I suddenly felt very frail. My legs were weak, like they could not hold up my body. My heart was beating very fast, and my breathing was so fast that I thought I would pass out. I sat on my bed with my head down for a few moments, feeling very ashamed of what I had done. I couldn't believe I had actually wanted to die. I had to make it right, but I wasn't sure what would make my life right.

I headed out for the bus stop. My mind was carrying on a dialogue with some doctor about whom I knew nothing—not even his appearance. I did not know how you were to approach a psychiatrist. Would he want to put me on some medication? What if he wanted to put me in a *hospital?* I decided I would tell him I was fine today. I was just torn up over being rebuffed by my first lover.

The bus seemed to take forever to get to the bus stop. Finally, I boarded the bus and took a seat by the window so I could see the numbers on the buildings. I had no idea what building or how far down his office was. I watched and saw it would be quite a few blocks. Downtown.

As I looked at the old Victorian homes, now turned into apartment buildings, a great melancholy came over me. These people most likely did not even know their own neighbors. Who on this bus knew the night before I had tried to commit suicide? Or cared? What horrors were in their lives as they sat, silent and gazing blankly. How different from my hometown where people sat on the porches and waved on summer Sunday afternoons as the neighbors walked their dogs and children skipped down the sidewalk. Here, people seldom even spoke—except maybe for a smile or a "hello." My town was a mining town. When the sirens went off it meant there was an accident in the mines. Everyone would go outside and wait for news of who was involved, or what was involved. Great fear struck our hearts.

If there was a death, food was brought by all. Comfort was given. Almost the whole town showed for the viewing, and all who knew the deceased appeared at the funeral. My mother said, "A small town takes care of its own." Here, only the small circle of influence responded to a tragic event. In fact, it was not considered tragic unless the news picked it up. If a person was a dignitary, or there were multiple people involved there would be a community reaction—to an extent. The pain of daily life was largely ignored. Except for the persons immediately affected. But, then who in my town knew of the violence in my home? What did I know about what went on in a home three blocks away? What was life really like there?

Ah! This was the stop. I got off and looked for the building. The Heyburn building. This was it. The swing doors led to a lobby facing the elevator. Not exactly a modern building, but had a polished look. Dr. Ehrler. Twelfth floor. I pushed the button and waited impatiently for the elevator. I got off on a carpeted hallway and followed the arrows to his office. A plain gold plaque displayed his name. I entered, my heart racing.

I was surprised for there was no one in the waiting room. Two secretaries were doing business at the typewriter. When I entered, one of them looked up.

"May I help you?"

"I need to see Dr. Ehrler."

"Do you have an appointment?"

"No. This is urgent."

She stepped in a door to my right, and came out in a very short period of time. "He'll see you in just a few minutes."

This was not the busy of the office of a doctor of internal medicine or an ob/gyn. There was no one there in the waiting room but me. The secretary gave me some papers to sign. I filled them out. Fortunately, I had bought health insurance through the school that was offered when I registered. I was seventeen. Would he call my mother? Or, my father? No sooner had I finished the required papers when Doctor Ehrler appeared.

He was tall, good looking man with dark glasses and thick dark hair. He wore a suit and was extremely well groomed. He had command of himself— that was obvious. I had really expected some thin, wiry, nervous type of person. "Come in, please." His voice was deep, and he had the demeanor of one in authority. I managed a smile and followed him into his office.

There was a formidable desk between him and me. I sat on a leather couch that caused me to slide down and slump. There were very few objects on his desk. A framed picture faced him. There was a classy looking clock and a chart with a pen lying on it.

"Am I supposed to lie on this couch?" I asked, making a stupid attempt at humor.

"Just make yourself comfortable." I chose to sit and watch what was happening, as it happened."

"So what makes this visit urgent?"

"I tried to kill myself last night. Swallowed a bottle of aspirin. My ears are ringing so "I can barely hear."

"The ringing will go away. What made you take such a desperate action?"

"Lost lover."

"So you had sex, and he dumped you. Where you using any form of contraception?"

"Well, I, uh, we…."

"Look, either the guy wore of rubber, or …"

Put on the spot, I answered, "We used withdrawal."

That seemed to satisfy him, but at this point I was feeling extremely uncomfortable. I was looking down at my hands, playing with a diamond ring my dad and stepmother had given me for my high school graduation.

"How did you get my name?" He inquired.

"In the yellow pages." This made him laugh, and I was embarrassed. It was naïve on my part I suppose. I really had no idea of how to find a psychiatrist. He started asking me questions about my childhood, and I talked openly about the violence in our home. I talked about how I had not fit in with the crowd with whom my mother had wished I be a part. I gave him information about my accomplishments, my successes. I told him how often, however, I felt like an utter failure. I told him I was going to be a successful writer. I also told him I wanted to act. He sat listening, looking down instead of directly at me, and responded to nothing I said. I felt no warmth or understanding from him. In fact, all I felt was anxiety.

"Is there anything else that is bothering you?"

"I don't think I am a Christian anymore."

To this he responded, "Well, what is so earth shattering about that?"

I was shocked. What is so earth shattering about that? Until the past few months I had based my life on my Christian beliefs. Spirituality had given me strength to pull through the hardships of my childhood. To me, it was the only tool that never let you down. I had let myself down by not subscribing to my beliefs. I did not comprehend the difference between spirituality and religion. I was lost. Being the chameleon that I was, I tried not to show any reaction to his question. It never occurred to me that others would not find that as monumental as an earthquake. I waited for his next question.

"Were you ever molested as a child?"

This sent a shiver riveting through my spine. I had never told anyone about this. How did he suspect? Or, was he just fishing? This was the source of much guilt. This was something no one should know. I sat in silence.

"Well?"

"There was a man when I was eight."

I paused, wishing we could talk about the Girl Scouts, or my work at the Methodist Home for Dependent Children. He sat, not moving, waiting for me to go on.

"He would come and ask my mother if he could take me for a walk. He would take me to a corn field and . . . well, touch me . . . down there."

"When did it stop?"

"One afternoon he came walking up, and I ran to my room crying. My sister always protected my brother and I."

I stopped. Not sure I could go on. But, I found the composure to continue. "My sister came and said, 'Lynn, you don't have to walk with him.' She went and told him I wasn't going on any more walks with him."

"It was not your fault, you know. You were a small child. He was an adult."

I had carried that shame all these years. I can remember him pulling down my shorts and putting his finger "up there." I could not cry or scream. I felt it was my fault. I would think of it at night and hide my face in my pillow. I dreaded seeing that man coming down the block. Mother had said it was okay. Suddenly, I realized it was not my fault! This man was a monster! Then, I came back to the scene in the psychiatrist's office. Somehow I, at that point, hid this under a box in my mind and never thought about it again until I was almost forty.

"What is your father like?""He is an attorney. He calls me 'The Pooh.'"
"Has he ever abused you sexually?"

"No, no. He's not like that. He would never do that."

"Where is your father?"

"He's here in Louisville. He's remarried. Mother and Dad divorced when I was three or four. That's how I got to western Kentucky."

"Well, we have to move on. Feel free to come back when you need to."

"What is wrong with me?"

"Ever heard of manic depressive psychosis?"

"Yes."

"Well, I think that is what is causing such drastic mood swings, and your constantly changing perspectives." He stood and opened the door, and no one had to tell me that was the cue to leave. "Come back when you need to," he said as I left. No one said anything about any fees. I did not know if they would bill my father, my mother, or me, but, I was in a hurry to get out and away. I noticed my hands trembling and felt cold and nervous.

On the way home I replayed all that had transpired. Manic depressive! That meant I was mentally ill! In a way, I was glad I had a diagnosis. It explained things. It meant there was a reason I behaved the way I did. He had said nothing about medication or hospitalization. What a relief! At least Room would feel the responsibility was off her.

My mood suddenly lifted. I was happy to be returning to the dorm. Maybe everything would change. Leo would come back. There would be more activity in the theatre. My creative writing would continue. I felt excited and hopeful again.

I got off at the stop near the university, and practically ran back to the dorm. None of the drama of the last 24 hours seemed important. I couldn't wait to tell Room I actually had a diagnosis.

It wasn't long before semester break and Christmas. I returned to my mother and brother and my hometown. My sister had married and moved to New Jersey. My friends were home and I visited with them, but I felt like a stranger. So much had happened. I was depressed. My church, my friends, all seemed surreal and distant. Room had returned for Christmas to Connecticut. I only wanted to get back to the dorm. To my life as I now knew it. Difficult as it was, I had a great desire to see how it played out. The small town life seemed drab, lifeless, and left me wondering, what, in fact, I did believe about the mysteries of life. This was no longer what I wanted. I did not want to "marry a nice guy and return home." The people were "country people" in my eyes at this point. I was mentally ill. Even if I did return to this, I was odd, different.

Registration for the second semester went smoothly. I was taking another creative writing class with the woman I had met my first day in the dorm, Nickie. I became very involved in the class and made friends with Nickie. There was something different about her on which I could not put my finger. We would be talking, and she would suddenly change the subject. Her major was psychology, but she was also a poet. There was strong, strong emotion in her poetry, and often a reference to the bizarre. Finally, I posed the big questions.

"Do you get depressed often?"

"Yeah. A lot."

"Have you ever seen a psychiatrist?"

"Every two weeks."

"Me, too, not every two weeks, but when I want to talk."

"Do you ever do this?" She asked, pulling up her sweater and showing red cuts, parallel on her white arms.

I looked with interest, but oddly found something enticing about that. "No, but I've overdosed."

These cuts were intriguing. I had to ask, "What do you do it with?"

"A razor blade."

This information was consciously stored in my memory for "emergency use" in the future. At this point in time, I was somewhat attracted to the world of the insane. My creative writing class encouraged me to delve into different ways of looking at things. I explored the delusional glass ball of ideas I had clung to for most of my life and expressed this exploration honestly in my poetry. My works were often discussed in our small class, and one even had written by the professor of the class, "Wow, Lynn!" It was the writing of one about to break.

I did not stop being actively involved in the community theatre, either. I tried out for a play requiring a teenage girl. I got a leading role. Who was opposite me? Glenn. He would have done an excellent job of bringing out my ability to act, but the director dropped him and two others for not learning their lines soon enough. Glenn was deeply angry and hurt when I did not walk out when he was dropped. But, I was full of manic, grandiose images of myself on the stage, and I simply did not have it in me to walk out.

The new young man working opposite me was flat and inept. I was simply interested in being on the stage. In two of the scenes I wore an evening gown, and I was excited about being *seen*. I had no experience as an actress, and I am sure my performance was lacking in depth and characterization. In fact, when opening night came, Leo came, and he made sure he let me know that the show was a flop, in his eyes. He told me I should see him in the show in which he was now performing. I was disappointed, but not in my performance; I was new at this. I was disappointed at his insensitivity. His face showed the scorn he had for me. Leo, commented that I needed to *study* acting, and that, as a matter of fact, I should see his performance in the Children's Theatre to see what acting was about. His face showed the scorn he had for me. Waiting. I had been waiting for him to come around. It became clear he was completely detached from any emotion but contempt for me.

Nevertheless, I thoroughly enjoyed the two weeks the show ran. I received dozens and dozens of roses on opening night. Between scenes I did my school work, and I dismissed any thought that there was something very sick going on inside me. Often, alone, the despair would surface. I wanted to explore it, not only in my poetry, but in the way I lived my life. I didn't look at self-destructive behavior as "acting out" any more than walking out in the sunshine was "acting out" the desire to feel the warmth of the golden ball in the sky. Both were based on engaging in life based on the knowledge and abilities I had at the time.

The semester came to an end, and I went home for two short weeks. I had decided to go to summer school to avoid being at my former home. I had met Jim Quine, who romanticized relationships to the point where they only existed in his fantasies. We were to have a summer romance. At the end of the summer, he would go back to his wife. After the relationship was over, I was not to try to contact him. He brought me flowers and read me his poetry. He was not interested in my poetry and considered me less in talent and ability than himself. All of these male artists seemed to think highly of themselves and look down on my talents, my abilities.

Once again, I lived in the land of hope and denial. I thought he would fall in love with me and decide to stay. I was consistently choosing relationships that had no future, and rejecting those that could have led to real affection and companionship. Did it ever occur to me to pay attention to how a person presented themselves upon first meeting them? I always, I suppose, thought I could "make it work," even though time after time, from early in the relationship—with whomever I was involved—I would disbelieve what I saw and heard and would listen to "but I will never hurt you." It took years before I learned that what you see is what you get, and if I chose what I saw, I had to accept the person for what they were instead of trying to force them into an image I *wanted* them to be. I had to learn that *one cannot make another being be anything other than what they are and change is the choice of each individual.*

I bought a pack of single edged razor blades and put them under my panties in the top drawer in the dorm room. Despair, that feeling of complete helplessness to control any aspect of one's life, was taunting me, relentlessly, savagely. I would take the package out and look at it occasionally, and then put it back. I took the step of getting the blade out of the package. Looking at the blade brought a surge of adrenalin to my body. The right moment would come.

Jim took me to Fountain Ferry Park. He had the idea that the ultimate in romantic thrills in our relationship would be riding the roller coaster with me. I went along with him, as I went along with life. To do nothing is choosing to do something. Youth, ignorance and inexperience allowed me to feel there was nothing, *nothing*, I could control. The roller coaster of Fountain Ferry Park was representative of my life. Up and down, around, then up and down senselessly, with no getting off once the trip was in motion. The joyride was a death ride. We experience many such deaths within our brief lifetimes. As we lose someone we love, we die. As we let go of habit, a good habit or a bad habit we die. We are no longer the same person with the same desires. Oh, on that roller coaster I wanted off. I promised God I would never get on another roller coaster if he would save me from this one. I no longer wanted thrills. I wanted off. I did not think in terms of where I might go instead of the path I was choosing. The path had me in its grips because I was aware of no other options. My skills at navigating the currents of Life were very, very limited.

The roller coaster did not crash, but I did. I sobbed, not so much from the ride, but from the realization of for what I was being used. This man, living out some romantic fantasy he had about a summer romance, was destroying what was left of a real human life. I had him take me back to the dorm, and I sat motionless on the bed for some time. Maybe a couple of hours.

Then I went to the drawer and pulled out the blade. I was not shaking or anticipating pain. I was in actuality quite detached from the whole experience. I did not want to make a suicide attempt. I wanted to feel the blade and see the blood.

I, being right handed, made a small red line on my left arm. The blood was so alive, so red. I felt almost dizzy with relief. I. More than I had in a long, long time. I had a washcloth and bandage ready. Part of the relief and thrill was tending to the wound. I washed it carefully with alcohol and put a gauze pad and adhesive tape on the negligible wound. I had been prepared for this for some time. I pulled down my sleeve and walked to a nearby restaurant for supper. Where was the point at which I could have controlled this behavior?

It very soon became an addiction—a temporary fix for the depression. It also had its own exculpatory facets. I was showing my sin in my own blood. I was performing an act of penance. I had traveled farther and farther away from my hometown, my beliefs about what was right and what was wrong. There was no forgiveness in my heart for myself. No compassion. No understanding.

Lunacy

a gnarled old woman
lies strapped
in the seclusion room
next to mine

lunacy, I ask,
is it governed
by the moon?
did it originate
in the synapse?
the Big Bang?

or, does
it come quietly,
like spilled ink

and touch
with only a finger
to make one black spot?

Sister, let me embrace you,
your life is slipping away.

Chapter Six

Highland Medicine

After the addiction to cutting began, it, as classically addictions do, became more frequent and more intense. Whenever I felt any kind of extreme emotion, I went to the drawer for a new blade, more gauze, and adhesive tape. The blood made me feel "real," or sometimes it took away what I called "brain pain" which was a mental anguish beyond description. The pain and blood brought temporary relief. At first there was cutting rarely. It became more frequent, and the cuts became a little deeper each time. I wore long sleeves to hide the marks. New ones were appearing before the old had time to heal.

Jim Quine left, and there was nothing to distract me. I was in the dorm waiting for the fall semester. Uncharacteristically, I decided to cut the top of my arm. It was a quick slash. The muscle was exposed. I needed stitches. I had to go to the emergency room if it was to get stitches. I think more than anything, I was ready to surrender to the illness, whatever happened to me. I was tired of hiding, tired of going from diversion to diversion. I did not want to walk around aimlessly anymore. I wanted something different. *What was it I was looking for?*. I did not know what the hospital could do, but was it not the place where people with mental afflictions went to heal?

I decided to go to the resident assistant on the floor. She was an upper class student who was there to assist when there was a problem, or roommates were not getting along. I went down the door and stopped. Did I really want this? Would not the wound heal on its own? I felt I could stand no more, and suicide was again becoming an option in my mind.

Room and I had nicknamed the resident assistant "RA." We had such a light-hearted relationship with her. Was she who was now the person in whom I put my fate? Of course not, I had been walking towards this moment every step, every choice, every misguided attempt to move in a different direction. I had missed the importance of the real tasks, the walking every day to meals, the everyday care of myself, the feeling of the sun, the cold, the rain trickling across my face. The real things that made up my life to which I was oblivious. Here I was at RA's door. Expecting someone else to make it all better. I hesitated as I lifted my fist to her door and then, finally, I knocked. The stamp on the envelope In a moment she opened the door.

"RA, I have a problem."

"What is wrong?"

"I have cut myself."

"Let me see."

"Did you do this intentionally?"

"Yes."

"You have other cuts that are older. How long has this been going on?"

"All summer."

"I'll have to call the dorm director. Come in and sit down."

I sighed when she said that for a number of reasons. It was the finality of the situation. It was the fact that the dorm director had to know, and who knows who else. My family would know. My father was out of town. What if they called my mother?

The resident assistant called the dorm director, who was out of town. This was a relief to me. RA said she would take me to the hospital. I liked RA and was glad she would be going with me. I knew the focus would be on my psychological state, but the cut did have to be stitched.

I sat in silence as we drove. I was having one of those internal dialogues with the doctor like I would often do when going into a situation. I can tell you with a one hundred percent certainty that these dialogues never went as planned. It was a mere waste of time. A way to still anxiety or slow down my thought processes. A way to become the one in charge.

I did not have to wait in the ER. They immediately took me back. A doctor came and looked at my arm. "Why have you been doing this?"

"I don't know." This was a partial truth. It took me years and years to really understand the dynamics of this behavioral and mental problem.

"Apparently, you have been doing this for some time. I am not worried about the cut. I am worried about what is going on in your head." I listened without responding.

"I will have to contact your parents."

"My father is on vacation. You absolutely cannot call my mother."

"Are you seeing a psychiatrist? Or, a therapist?"

"I see Dr. Ehrler sometimes."

"I'll give him a call."

It seemed like a very long time before he returned. Perhaps he was seeing other people, also. I had never been in an ER before. There was much buzzing activity. I became resigned to whatever happened.

When the doctor returned, he informed me that he and Dr. Ehrler would send me to Highland Medicine until my father returned, and arrangements from there would be determined. He told me they would send me there by ambulance.

I was surprised by the sterile environment of the psychiatric unit. All the staff wore white, including a male orderly. The RN's and LPN's wore caps; the LPN's one stripe; the RN'S two. My vital signs were taken and I was shown around the unit by Paula, a nurses' aide. It looked like any other hospital unit, except instead of waiting rooms, there was a community room with comfortable sofas and tables with chairs.

"This room serves as a community room and dining area. Often, at night, the patients play cards or board games," Paula explained. She was very stiff and never smiled. It was impossible to determine what sort of personality was cloaked under that uniform. I was shown my room, a double room with only two beds and a dresser. There were no comforts of any kind. It was a barren womb.

She introduced me to some of the other patients, and I immediately noticed they were almost all older than I. There was one young woman who seemed to be lost in her own head and did not respond to the introduction. Otherwise, they were ordinary people, it seemed. There was a formidable looking locked area in the back of a long hall, which I dismissed from my mind as something I would rather not know about. All I knew was that there was a sign above the heavy door that said "Acute."

I took note of the comfortable areas on the unit. The community rooms were lit with regular table lamps, so the areas did not have the institutional look of overhead fluorescent lighting. There were not phones in the rooms, but there were two community phones. I was given the numbers when admitted. Supper came at five o'clock precisely. I was told I would be given a menu after dinner so I could choose what I wanted for the next day.

After dinner Dr. Ehrler appeared. "What do you think of the unit?"

"It's okay.'

He was brief. "I'll order something if you need it for sleep. Just ask for it at the nurses' station."

I tried to reach out to some of the other patients. There was one man—he was an elderly man—who was particularly nice. He was there for depression. He said he was trying a new medication tonight.

I found out quickly everyone wanted to talk about what their doctor had said that day. The doctor was the king pin. I also found out quickly I did not get much information from my doctor. Therapy was not about talking; it was about meds and getting along with the staff. I was put on a number of medications, including Seconal for sleep, something for anxiety, I don't remember what else. At some point I remember being put on antipsychotics, but the need for that was never explained to me. Interesting, because years later I read the results of the psychological tests they gave me. Interesting, because I was diagnosed, according to the psychological tests they gave me, with a severe dissociative disorder. I don't know why they would have given me meds for psychosis, unless they did not trust their own diagnosis. The medication intensified the feeling I had that I was dreaming. I can tell you that. I remembered the experience as being in a dream-like state with people floating to me and then floating away.

It was all too easy to fall into the "comfort" of the hospital structure. One adapted to being treated as an object with which to be reckoned. I don't know how long I would have chosen to stay there if money was not an issue. I got stuck in a pattern that was unhealthy and dysfunctional. Far more dysfunctional, in fact than what I had left to come here. Meals were served at eight, twelve, and five. If your behavior was acceptable, you had access to the arts and crafts rooms from ten in the morning until shortly before lunch, and again in the afternoon. Bedtime was at eleven, and the lights were out and you were expected to be in bed. "PRN'S"were good for boredom. There were no groups to discuss what brought one to the hospital, and how a person could find better ways to cope with life outside the hospital. The focus was coping with life inside the hospital. Alignments were made with others who had similar problems to the ones that had brought them to the hospitl. Alcoholics sought other alcoholics. Depressed persons sought people sympatihetic to their issues—if they sought anyone. In the community area, patients got in small groups and discussed what their psychiatrist had said in the short time he or she (usually he) spent assessing the patient's progress with the patient.

I made an unlikely friendship with a man in his sixties. He was severely depressed, and the medications did not seem to working. We would talk about how our families were reacting to our treatment or side effects of our medication.

One evening he seemed particularly depressed. This was my first week of hospitalization, and I did not really know much about him. I asked him the usual questions, but he seemed distracted. From what I understood, he had been their some time. Evidently, he either had excellent insurance, or he was wealthy. I was concerned, and I asked him what had him so down.

"My wife wants a divorce."

"Why?"

"She's tired of dealing with my hospitalizations."

"But, you cannot help it if you are depressed!"

I had heard his daughter had been killed in an automobile accident a year ago, but he had never told me. I was guarded in what I said.

"You don't understand. She's been very patient until now. Says she's tired of dealing with my depression. She thinks all I care about is myself."

"Oh, I'm so sorry!"

"Thanks. I don't feel like talking right now."

"Okay. I'll let you think things over."

I went to my room and started crying, and not just for him. I knew eventually my family, and my psychiatrist for that matter, would tire of my problems. What would happen when I had to leave the hospital? I couldn't think about that! I just couldn't! I felt my heart beating faster, and I felt scared and helpless. The thought came to my mind that there were light bulbs in the lamps in the community room. I desperately wanted to slash through an artery and try to die. I couldn't tell the nurses. No, I could tell them, but I did not want to. I wanted control. This seemed like a way to control what happened to me. It would be my decision—not the decision of fate.

I had to get in the community room when no one was looking. I went to survey the situation. I sat in one of the chairs. My friend was gone, and there was only one woman playing solitaire. Could she please leave? I looked impatiently through a magazine. Finally, she left. I hurriedly unscrewed the bulb and headed for my room. There was no one sharing the room with me at this time. I had the opportunity. At this point I felt there was no turning back. I was committed to the act.

I went in my room, and, after grabbing some towels from the vanity I went to the bath. The towels would muffle the sound of breaking glass. I wrapped up the bulb and stomped it. There was a slight pop. I knew the bulb was broken. I chose a piece of glass and paused for a second. Then I slashed my left wrist deep enough to hit an artery. Blood was pulsing out. I stood watching the blood dripping off my wrist. And I waited.Every fifteen minutes or so the aides would check on the patients. I wasn't bleeding enough. I slashed the other wrist. Then I panicked. There was a knock on the door.

"Lynn, are you in there?" It was Paula. "Lynn?" The door opened. I looked up, and Paula switched an "emergency" lever on the wall next to the shower.

Paula's flat affect matched mine. I was wheeled to the ER, sown up, and very shortly got to see that area with the sign "Acute" above it. I was given special white pajamas, and I was told I would sleep in the second room. There were five rooms arranged in a semi-circle, and the nurses' station extended into acute. However, communication with the nurses was controlled through a sliding, thick glass window. The rooms had only one bed; there were no furnishings. I watched them put my belongings in a closet next to my room.

A nurse with two stripes on her cap approached me through a door that lead from the nurses' station to the acute area. There was a small area between the rooms and the nurses's confined area. The door I had entered remained closed and locked.

"Why did you do this, Lynn?"

"Because I hate myself."

"What did you hope to accomplish?"

Knowing they would only see this as a bid for attention, I answered, "I wanted to see the blood." No matter what answer I could have given, I thought, it would not be acceptable

The nurse said, "Here, take this." She held out a pill and a glass of orange juice.

"No, thank you," I replied.

"You don't have a choice. It's either you take it, or we give it to you by injection."

As she left, I went and lay down on my bed. A window covered with wire mesh viewed an entrance to the hospital. There was no way the window could be opened, as far as I could see. A sparrow flew by, and I followed it to the sky. I got up again, somewhat fuzzy from whatever she had given me, and looked to see who else was confined here. I had never seen anyone come in or out of this section.

There were only two other patients on the unit. There were no closed doors on this section at this time, so it was easy to ascertain. A gnarled old lady approached me. "Honey," she said, "lunacy is governed by the moon."

"Pardon me?" I asked, somewhat taken aback.

"Yes it comes quietly."

"Why do they have you back here?"

"Where?"

"Why are you in this section?"

"This section of what?"

"The hospital . . . the psych unit?"

"Oh...the hospital .... They said something about dementia. Dammit. I can't find my purse!" She then went and started pounding on the window of the nurses' station. "I can't find my driver's license! Dammit! I said I can't find my driver's license!"

Finally, a nurse came to the window. "Mrs. Burnett, we have it locked up for you. Now go lie down." She closed the window and went back to her paper work.

The woman was not satisfied and pounded again on the glass partition. "My husband's coming, and he'll get me out of here. He's gonna' drive me to the airport. I have a plane to catch in two hours. If you don't let me go, I'll suit you! I may be old, but I have rights!" Over the years I found it was useless to threaten to suit any staff for any reason. Patients claimed often of abuse, but seldom were the comments even acknowledged.

When she saw that demanding her rights was not getting her what she wanted, she started whining. "Honey, now, please give me my things. I don't know where any of them are. Help me find them." Finally, she ambled away to a bed—not her own—and sat and mumbled to herself.

The other patient on Acute was an aged gentleman, bedridden, who barely made himself known. He lay, glazed eyes seemingly fixed on the single bulb on the ceiling in his room. It was a sad sight, and was, as in Buddhist terminology, a Heavenly Messenger. A reminder of how time moved on forward, and we all faced the same sword, eventually. I felt a piercing fear as I watched him. What was my life becoming? Why was a wasting precious moments in a damn cell? It was by choice, in a way. But, somehow my wrung out mind could not deal with this . . . at least not now.

I removed myself as best I could from the situation. I huddled in the corner of my room. I began to be aware of angels singing. I sat and rocked back and forth. These unbidden voices were soothing. The walls and doors became distorted, and the sound of Mrs. Burnett became a hum. I could hear her wailing and banging against the window in the nurses' station. The troops came in, and I heard them drag her off, wailing and crying. However, I did not feel any emotion, for myself, for her, for the world. I listened to the angels and rocked.

While I was on Acute, Dr. Ehrler made short visits daily. "You know your refractory behavior landed you here."

"What exactly is refractory behavior?"

"You are not being compliant with treatment."

"What treatment?" It was an innocent question, in truth. I mean, I had painted some tea pots and was working on an oil painting. To what treatment was he referring? But, the question made him very obviously angry. He threw down his arms, looked up at the ceiling, and turned to walk away. I shrugged.

Finally, after I don't know how many days, he came and said I was being moved to the main unit. And, I would be administered ECT. Shock treatments. It was not asked if I consented or did not consent. It was made as a statement. Most of the people who were being treated there and remained for more than two weeks received them, so I assumed it was standard operating procedure.

The night before my first treatment, I was told to shower and put on pajamas that were like the ones worn in Acute. An N.P.O. sign was posted on my door. Before they took me to the Treatment Room, they gave me a shot. "Your mouth will get dry," the two striped nurse told me.

I did not know what to expect. I knew they put you out when you received them, but I had seen patients after they had received them. They could not remember what had happened the day before the treatment. It was not inhumane, but I was angry because no one had asked me if I would agree to them. I became stoic and resigned to whatever was my fate. I received three treatments a week for a period of weeks. I cannot now remember how many I received, but I do remember one in which I balked at the forced treatment.

I went to the nurses' station and flatly refused anymore treatments. I was told I would have to tell Dr. Ehrler that. So I did. He came to my door and said, "What is this? You say you will not receive any more E.C.T."

"No." There was a nurse standing by his side. "Would you grab one arm, please? Shall we?" With that they literally began dragging me fighting and screaming down the hall. Then I stood up to walk. When their grip was released I ran down the hall. An orderly picked me up, all 95 pounds of me, and carried me to the Treatment Room. There I submitted to whatever the hell they wanted to do with me. As I went under, I said, "Goodbye."

little man

you can smell
the institution
the walls sweat
the earth around cries,
"Love me, God,
now love me!"

so love
the little man
who prays,
his brimmed hat,
pajama shirt,
his coat and tie
"I'm going crazy,"
said the man,
"so love me."

so love him, God,
so love him

Chapter Seven

Love Me

And goodbye it was. For years after I was admitted to the state hospital, I could remember only the tiniest bit of what had happened at Highland Medicine. One psychologist told me until I got over "this big fat case of amnesia" I could expect to stay in a state mental hospital." However, once I was admitted to L7, all that existed was this institution. In fact, until Bev came, there existed nothing but this unit and survival. I did as I was told. I did not speak. I took my tray at meal time and pretended to eat. I did not wish to be anywhere else. There was nowhere else.

I was approached by the doctor one morning. "Here. Sign this." I had no idea what he wanted me to sign. "You do not want to go to the court, do you?" I did not have the faintest idea of what court or where and what going to court would mean. I took the pen and signed the paper. I had signed an agreement to be treated by the hospital. The paper was an alternative to being committed by the court to the hospital. Or, possibly, to be released from the hospital if I was not an immediate threat to myself or someone else or was psychotic. Was I a threat to myself? In the sense I had nowhere to go, had no contact with anyone outside of the hospital, yes. I would have wandered into homelessness. So, I suppose, the agreement was a good thing. This was the late sixties. Deinstitutionalization was in its beginnings. Chronic patients who knew no home but the hospital were given a bus ticket and sent to the community with no resources.

Interestingly, I later read the notes written by this doctor. "This patient is not to be made a pet by the staff." This explained a lot. Something about me made me like a pet. Was it my age? My childlike naivety? The staff definitely did not treat me like a pet, but I was very young, attractive, and bright. I was creative and had potential. In the end these qualities probably saved me from the "back wards" that still existed.

I don't know how long it was until Bev appeared. It may have been days. It may have been weeks. She made a lot of noise as they brought her on the unit. I was aghast. Here was a young woman whose face had flesh hanging from it. She was gaunt and her skin was sallow. She looked like pictures I had seen of concentration camp victims. "Please, please, send me back to B2! I promise—I promise to do whatever I'm told!"

"Maybe tomorrow," they replied, "depending on how you act tonight. If you pull any of your stunts, you will be here a month."

I watched her pacing the floor crying. "Can I have some crackers and juice?"

"Look, Bev," an exasperated nurse answered, "You eat when everyone else does. Ask again and you will do without supper."

"Why don't they feed her?" I thought. "This poor woman is starving to death."

I stayed at a distance, but once in the community room she cornered me. "What is your name?"

"Lynn."

"Do you have anything to eat?"

"No one here has food."

"They won't give me anything to eat."

"Why?"

"I don't know....why don't you ask to come to B2? It's much nicer than this. I hate L7. I hate it here. They won't give me anything to eat."

I was baffled by this, but had learned a valuable piece of information. There was a better place to be in this institution—B2. Bev and I had no other words, and she left the next day.

A few days later the doctor called me in his office. "How are you, Mees Lynn?" he asked in his thick accent. I nodded my head, which was not an answer, but was all I could muster.

He cocked his head sideways as if trying to ascertain my state of mind.

"How do I get to B2?" I blurted out.

"You have to talk, talk to the other pateents. You have talked to no one."

I was now a woman with a mission. I found a woman, who though she did not give answers to my questions, looked as though she was conversing with me. Suddenly, I recognized her. She was the woman with the faux fur coat in the paddy wagon! I felt that I had found an old friend. The memory of the paddy wagon came back. I was glad she was at least safe. I wondered what had landed her on this unit. She talked quite oddly. Kept asking me, "Where is my dog? Where is Sniff?" This was disturbing because I had no idea where she was from or, for that matter, anything about her. I imagined her dog stuck in an empty house, starving and thirsty. *No! I can't think about that!* I could not let myself be pulled into a vacant field of sorrow for all of us, myself included, in this virtual prison. I listened to her. "It's about time for me to go .." sne said. I realized her purpose in talking to me was quite different than my purpose of listening to her. I began trying to listen—really listen to the pain without immersing myself in her rattling closet of bones and bits and pieces of tattered tales of a life she once had.

But, my original purpose in entertaining her ramblings was met. Several days later an aide came and said I was being transferred to B2. She gave me clothes I had forgotten I had owned. The guard was waiting to transfer me. He was making some flirtatious remarks to the staff. When he saw me, he commented, "Damn, we're getting them younger and younger."

Then there was the rattling of the keys. I took one long look down the hall and then followed the guard out the door. I had no idea where B2 was. I looked out a barred window and saw a gentle snow falling. We went to the elevator, and it clanged as the elevator approached the floor.

As we entered for some reason he set everything down. He locked the elevator somehow. *What now?* The lecherous look was unmistakable in his eyes. He pushed me against the wall of the elevator. I smelled the foul odor of urine that had marked my first entrance into this tin can. He felt my breasts. I blacked out. I had a similar blackout while riding a feisty horse at Girl Scout Camp. We were riding down a sunny path and the horse took off across a weedy field. The next thing I remember was one of the camp counselors had ahold of the bridle on my horse. I was told the horse had jumped over a three-and-a-half foot fence and I went with him like a pro. I have no memory of this.

After being cornered in the elevator, the next thing I remember I was being on a new unit in a modern building and the staff was crowded around the guard. One of the male staff shoved him. I was, strangely, left to the side by myself crying, grappling with whatever it was that happened.

Things were moving in slow motion in my mind. The guard left and the staff started handing out trays. It was supper time. There was real meat and a cupcake with white icing! I looked out the window and could see the old building in the distance. *Nothing really bad happened in that elevator. I would remember. At least this is a decent place to stay.* There was Bev! She was sitting alone. Over the course of several days, I learned she was required to eat alone.

After dinner Bev was ordered to sit in the community area and not to get up. It was not true she was not given food. What was her story? I was finally given a room by the nurses' station. There were two beds. One was empty. Curtains covered the large windows. It was delightful to be out of L7. This wasn't going to be bad, after all, now that I was off that prison unit. One of the staff brought me a box full of clothes that I recognized as my own, but I could not figure out where they had been. It was like Christmas having a nice wardrobe again. Over the next few weeks, I began to write poetry again. There was a lot of time. I was given a notebook so I could keep them together. There were older poems in a cardboard stationary box with my clothes.

There was one visitor who came during this early time on B2. but I did not recognize him until thinking about him much later, when my memory started coming back. It was the gentleman who befriended me at Highland Medicine. He knew my name, and could not understand what had happened to me. "My God! What have they done to you?" Not being able to recollect how I got there, I could not begin to answer that question.

He asked if he could come from time-to-time to visit me. Because I did not even know who he was or why he was visiting, I told him that was not wise. A psychologist who had made the unasked for statement about my "fat" amnesia asked if this man was my "Sugar Daddy." I told him since I had a "fat" amnesia. I had no way of knowing.

At first I was not allowed off the unit. Until it was believed you were safe and would not run away from the hospital, you were kept on the unit. The doors were locked that led off the unit, but they were not the heavy metal doors I had seen in the old building. I had no desire to run away. I had no idea how I would survive. My family was not writing, calling, or contacting me in any way. Who were my friends before I landed here, I could not remember. No one visited.

Periodically, I would start crying hysterically. I did not know why or even what I was feeling. The tears would come and I would shake violently. I was usually given an injection of a drug that would make me sleep for several hours.

Among my belongings was a book of poems *Drowning with Others*. I did not remember where I had obtained this paperback book. I liked the poems. I put the book in the window in my room behind the curtain. An aide noticed it when checking my room. This is routine in all the psychiatric units on which I have ever been. The Keepers look for anything sharp or lighters—contraband.

"Who put that up there?"

"I don't know," I said, and she simply laid it on my metal bedside table.

This, I thought was the problem with the way the institution treats the patients. It is the way we ALL treat each other, staff and patients alike. We ARE all drowning—and drowning together. Death is ever present, but we never talk about it. We are not supposed to talk about it. How can we deal with this inevitability if we could not even discuss ways of dealing with that large beast that followed us around our whole damn lives? Here I was at age eighteen in a state mental hospital indefinitely. We can't breathe Life. We can't be out doing what is normal. What is normal? I began to feel a surge of depression. But, I knew better than to talk about it. I wrote many a poem about my depression. There was no one I trusted, though. I did cry sometimes, but I did not talk. Most of what I cried about was about the lost memories of what had brought me here. The scars were there, but I did not know how they got there.

I found out early that my mother had lied when she told me to quit worrying about death at age four when I asked her when I was going to die. She had said people die when they get old. My friend, Anne, two years my junior, had a brother who was the same age as I named Jimmy. But, Jimmy did not play with us because he was sick and mostly read comic books and stayed in his room. When I was allowed to go to Mass with Anne's family, Jimmy always went but, other than that, he was a presence that was more like a ghost. Jimmy had cystic fibrosis.

I loved to forage through his enormous collection of comic books at one stage in my childhood. His favorite was *Superman*. He had other books and toys, but he stayed mainly to himself. I even took to spending my allowance to buy comics I shared with him. But, he was not particularly interested in my comics about Superwoman, the female counterpart. I thought Kryptonite was a wonderful play on the element Krypton. The superpower's susceptibility to Kryptonite seemed based on logic. And I believed one day he would be well.

We accepted his illness as part of his life and part of ours. Then, at age twelve, he went in the hospital and stayed a long, long time. Anne and I did not talk about it until after she and her other brother, Michael, were taken to the hospital to see him.

"How is Jimmy," I asked when she came home that afternoon.

"His stomach looked all funny. It was so big."

Something seemed terribly wrong, but I did not pursue it with Anne. She was as playful and spritely as always. Instead, I went to Mother. "Why was his stomach all swollen," I asked.

"Jimmy is dying," she explained. I walked off wondering how someone so young could be taken by a God who was supposed to be loving. Jimmy knew. He knew all along. Superman, his hero, beat the odds. He would not. Jimmy was *my* hero. I could not fathom the strength this child had.

The next day when I went to school, two of his cousins who were in my class were sitting at a table crying. "Lynn, Lynn, come here! Be with us! Jimmy is going to die!"

I remember being touched that they acknowledged that I had a very special bond to this family. We hugged each other and wept.

On Saturday my mother called me from work. "Lynn, Jimmy died. I am very sorry. You don't have to go to school Monday. We will go to his funeral." Then her words trailed off, and I went to lie down on my bed. I buried my head in my pillow, lying there not knowing what I felt. There were no tears. Just a terrible loneliness like I had never experienced.

My sister came to the door of my room and said, "Lynn, you are not the only one who is sorry Jimmy died." I did not know what she was trying to say, so I did not respond. I, as so often I reacted when I did not understand, was silent.

My mother took me to the funeral home for the visitation. It was just the two of us that came from my family. We sat near the back and I saw the heads of many people I did not know. I also saw a body in a casket. It did not look like Jimmy. I had never been in a room with a dead person before. In fact, I had never been in the room with a casket. I kept waiting for his chest to rise. I would think I was seeing it but, then, no, he was so, so still.

"Would you like to sign the guest register?" she asked me softly.

I nodded, "Yes."

She took my hand and we walked down to the register next to the body of Jimmy. I glanced at him and noticed he had purplish tinge. I was frightened. I was glad Mother was there. I never loved her more. She was kind and understood. It was obvious. She was sincerely caring. I signed my name beneath the long list of people who had come to pay their last respects.

I was friends with Anne for a long time after the death of her brother, but we seldom spoke of his death. I saw the staunch strength of her family …. Or perhaps….I didn't see what, in truth, the loss of a child had done to his parents. I don't know. I know for a long time I wanted to be Roman Catholic. I wanted the faith they seemed to have. I wanted that unbendable strength. They seemed to rely so strongly on their faith.

The fear of death and the grief intensified after Jimmy's death for a while. I prayed constantly for more faith. I wanted some sort of insurance that there was something more than just living each day, going to school. What for? After age fourteen or so, I became more interested in my social, school and other interests. The fear was put to the back of my mind, but it was there. It slipped into my conscious mind with odd triggers. I would look at a newborn baby, for example, and think, "You, too, will die."

When I was sixteen, a close girlfriend died—killed in a car accident. This was tragic, but it did not affect me the way Jimmy's death had. Jimmy was my brother.

But, here I sat in a state mental hospital, once again plagued by my own insignificance and a belief that we, as humans, were merely passing time until our death.

Finally, though, I was allowed to leave the unit. There was a canteen, and I had an account that I could use to buy sandwiches and soft drinks. I had not known I had account. I supposed my father had put the money in there. We had talked twice since I had been admitted here. But, he or my stepmother did not visit. No one visited. I didn't think about it too much. That was another life.

I was called to the office by one of the social workers. I was told we had the opportunity to do therapeutic tasks for a small amount of money that we could use in the canteen, or to buy items we needed for ourselves. I was assigned to a men's geriatric unit on L3 to work. I really had no idea what that would entail.

My first day there I found little would be expected of me. I stayed behind the nurses' station and drank tomato juice and ate saltines. A new taste for me. I had always rejected the offer of tomato juice. The unit was run by an LPN and two aides. When the LPN was not there, the aides would talk about how hateful and arrogant she was.

"Does she think that stripe on her cap makes her sergeant in charge of the Army," Bea asked Maria.

"She acts like she got a rod up her ass," Maria answered.

"I ain't pussy footin' around just to please her."

"We'll be sure and let her know," They cackled.

I observed all this, and more. I watched closely how they handled themselves and the patients. It was a dirty, filthy ward housing mainly demented gentlemen who knew little about what was going on in their world, much less the world outside of this unit.

One day, Bea was acting like she was crazier than any of the patients who I had seen in this institution. There was a slightly built man with hair loosely hanging down on his forehead. He came to the station repeatedly talking in a manner that to most people would probably have made little sense. Somehow I saw that he did feel; he did need to be cared for and treated with dignity. After repeatedly asking for a cigarette and being refused, he came one more time to the nurses' station. I looked at him, Benji, and noticed his plaid shirt was a pajama shirt. He wore loose pants, a jacket, a bowtie and a hat with a brim. I supposed they at least bathed and dressed these painfully childlike persons, aimlessly walking up and down the hall. The unit was much like L7 in physical appearance.

Because Bea and Maria were busy laughing and gossiping, I approached the counter and asked, "What's up, Benji?"

Poignantly, he answered, "I am going crazy, so love me."

"I do love you, Benji," I answered.

"Give me a cigarette," he pleaded, "Give me a cigarette."

"I don't have a cigarette. I don't smoke."

"I don't smoke," he parroted me.

Bea, who unbeknownst to me, had seen me talking to him. She grimaced and grabbed a broom. Get away from here!" She chased him down the hall, hitting him with the straw end of the broom.

I had never seen such disrespect of a helpless human being. I watched, stunned. Maria was holding her hands around her belly, laughing at Bea and Benji. Zip, as the LPN was called, came in at that point and the merriment at the expense of Benji stopped. I was still a withdrawn patient, even though I had more privileges now. I knew little of how this institution was run, but I made the decision at that point to risk going to the person who had assigned me to this unit. God, I hoped someone would at least take note of these lost old men.

I left and went back to my building. I sat a long time thinking. "What's wrong, Lynn?" asked a patient, seeing me sitting in the community room, quiet, not paying any attention to the room or who was in it. She sat beside me.

"Nothin'."

"Something is eating you."

"Nothin' you can help me with."

"Well, holler if you need me."

A new patient was being admitted. She was obese and had a shabby, tattered skirt and a blouse with rhinestones. The doctor was questioning here.

"Whew! You smell! Do you piss often?" The woman just looked at him.

"The word is urinate, Doctor," the nurse corrected him politely.

"Urinate, piss, void, what's the difference? Whew! What is that smell? Is it your pussy? Nothing ever smelt worse than a woman's pussy. Whew!"

This lovely interview that was heard all over the unit answered my question. The administration and clinical staff either did not know or did not care about the dignity of the question. I could not fight what was considered acceptable staff by …. Well, at least the administration and most of the other staff members who were under their supervision. There was no one I could trust. I felt very depressed and went to my room to lie down. I missed supper. I heard a ruckus about some dried vomit found in one of the trash cans. I heard bantering between the evening staff and Bev. Bev was apparently eating whatever she could get her hands on and then she would vomit. I did not understand this behavior, but then I did not understand the judgmental behavior of the staff, either. What I saw was a time that had not yet come, where mental illness was in fact considered an illness. Yes, they had the Medical Model which was supposed to be a guide to diagnosis and treatment. There were very little medications at this point. The early antipsychotics were helpful, but all too often used to restrain a patient rather than treatment.

We, at this institution, were often treatment instruments by facilities in the community—University of Louisville School of Medicine, University of Louisville Department of Psychology, and various schools that taught nursing. Most of the time, I enjoyed the staff that came from these schools, especially the Department of Psychology. They at least attempted to offer treatment.

The oddest thing was that you were expected to "help yourself," yet your diagnosis was kept as guarded secret, especially from you, the patient. It was under your control, and you damn well better control it. But, you were not told what it was. Manipulation was the pat answer for almost all behavior. I had yet to be put in any sort of group situation, and one on one counseling was only, on this unit anyway, done by these irregular visits from educational facilities.

Once a rather brazen doctor with students surrounding him, called me in for an interview. After the initial introductions and how are you doing part, the doctor put forth a question that made me wonder who in the hell this authoritative son of a bitch was.

"Are you a Lesbian?" There was no indication I was a Lesbian, not that I would have told him if I was. I have no problem with a person's sexual orientation, but I just didn't know who the hell this man thought he was. I thought to myself that he more than likely had read my history and thought he had me all figured out—incorrectly. I got up and left. As I was leaving, I heard him say, "We sure wiped the smile off her face!" Was that his goal?

As I walked out, I heard our unit's gracious doctor in a vehement discussion with a new patient. He was verbally assaulting her.

"YOU ARE A SOCIOPATH!"

"What have I done? You don't even know me!"

"I know you are a criminal!"

"I haven't been convicted of any crime!"

"I don't treat criminals. I am sending you off my unit!"

"Don't think I am going to cry about it."

The woman was escorted to another building with the same security guard who had brought me from L7. I knew so little about her, but soon would grow to know so much.

That day I went to see my social worker who had sent me to L3 to work. I was quite surprised at what she was talking to me about! She was talking about discharge. There was a possibility I could get back in school. The state would help with any expenses. But, I was not being discharged right away. A new doctor had a group that met on our unit, and she wanted me to attend for a while. In an off handed way, as I was leaving, she casually mentioned I would be reassigned in my occupational therapy. One of the staff had objected to a young girl being sent to work with a unit full of men.

I agreed to go to the group. I felt exhilarated and terrified. Yes, indeed, it was possible to get dependent on this hospital. I had not been off the grounds, and had lost touch with everyone I had known. I had no visitors. Not even my family. At least here there was some familiarity. It was predictably unpleasant.

The next day I went to the group to which I had been assigned. The group was led by a doctor from another unit. I went in and looked around. There was the woman who had been thrown off the B2! We went around the circle giving our first names. Her name was Martha. She was around my age and, as I came to find out as I grew to know her, had a wonderful sense of humor.

The doctor was a scraggly middle aged man. His shirt was thread bare and the buttons of his shirt were pulled apart by his large loose belly. His hair looked greasy and hung in strands across his forehead. His physical appearance was, in fact, slovenly.

So, the talking started. One of the doctor's favorite sayings was, "let it all hang out." Also, when patients would bring up the errors in judgment that led to their hospitalization here and try to justify it, he would snidely, cynically say, "Yeah, that's right your shit doesn't stink." I wanted this man's approval, just like I wanted the approval of anyone in authority.

People started talking about their shame. I talked about myself, and he said, "I think you are very sick. Schizophrenic, in fact." I have no idea why he said that to me. I was given so many diagnoses already that I really didn't care what he called me. The only thing I didn't want to be called was sociopathic. I knew I had empathy for people and a very strong sense of morality. But, these doctors were quicker to throw that diagnosis in your face than any other label.

It was obvious here that you were readily given one of two labels: schizo-phrenic or sociopathic. I found the label told very little of the person's story. It wasn't just that you HAD schizophrenia—you were in fact a different species—a schizophrenic.

The talking was interrupted when a group of staff members entered. We had to go through introductions again. The staff never talked, except for the leader. None of the staff I knew, but by sight. I could tell their presence changed the tone of the group. The members were more reticent.

After the group was dismissed, Martha came over to me. "Why don't you move to the unit I am on," she asked me.

The group doctor heard this, and he, too, approached me. His unit was in an older building, but the doors were unlocked, and you were allowed free-dom to come and go as you pleased during the day, until dark. The doctor said, "Would you like to come with us?"

Martha was quite persuasive. She talked about how friendly the people were. I had grown comfortable on B2, but Martha seemed like she could ac-tually be a friend. The group doctor approached my present physician, and I was given a choice whether to be transferred. I chose to transfer, mainly be-cause I saw the possibility of a friendship between Martha and me. I was aware I felt disloyal to the staff on B2. That, indeed, was sickness. These people were not my friends. They were Keepers.

This new unit was not modern or fancy. There were rows of beds in lines up and down the unit—a woman's unit. The doors were not locked, and some-how it seemed peaceful. There were huge windows. It was spring, and the smells of grass, freshly cut, brought the outside world inside.

Martha and I, soon after I had moved to this unit, were sitting outside the back of the unit on the fire escape. What a pleasant night it was! The air was balmy, and somewhere there were croaking frogs.

At first we discussed the type of things one discusses when first accus-toming oneself to a person. Martha had a decent job before "all this hap-pened." She had a roommate, Donna, who was pregnant with a child and no husband. Martha's life sounded no different than most people in the Hippy Movement—sexual freedom, recreational drugs, and a desire to look for something meaningful beyond Viet Nam or discrimination on gender or ethnic background.

"That doctor," she said, almost pleading, "he wouldn't even let me be a patient on his floor because he thinks I am a *sociopath.*"

"First of all," I began, "most of the doctors here aren't even psychiatrists. I happen to know his specialty is ob/gyn. Unless you are pregnant of have venereal disease, I wouldn't necessarily take stock in what he says."

Martha lit out a cigarette, and contemplated what I was saying. She blew her smoke out in long, deliberate exhales.

"Secondly," I continued, "half the people here are diagnosed as sociopaths, and the other half are diagnosed with some form of schizophrenia, with a few manic people thrown in like salt and pepper. My last statement is this—this is an insane asylum." I spoke enunciating the term "insane asylum" with great deliberation and a sardonic tone.

Martha caught my humor and chuckled. She added, "A looney bin."

"A *state* mental hospital." We started laughing at, I guess, was the absurdity of the institution .

"A cuckoo's nest!"

"A funny farm!"

"The nut house!"

We came up with as many names as we could for the place, and by this time we were in hysterics. Who would have thought we would meet in such a ludicrous environment? Lunatic asylum! What insanity just in the name! Yet the trees and the grounds held such peace this spring night.

"By the way," I started on a serious note, "how did you earn the title sociopath?"

"You know, the roommate I mentioned? Donna? You will meet her. She's bringing me some clothes. Well, we smoke some pot sometimes and I decided to try acid. It was fantastic! But, I shouldn't have dropped it alone.

Anyway, the colors were so beautiful! And I was seeing flames come out of things. But, I knew I was hallucinating. I decided that I would like some real fire. What an experience, I thought. So, I emptied out a metal trash can, which I think shows some wisdom for someone tripping, and I put some papers and clothes in it. I took it out on the balcony and lit it."

"Oh, shit!" I interjected as an editorial comment.

"The neighbors saw this. I mean it was the middle of the afternoon."

"Oh, of course."

"Anyway, they called the fire department and the police. I don't know what the fuck I said. I was tripping out of my mind. They took me to jail. The other women there quickly nicknamed me 'Psycho'. God only knows what I was saying or seeing. But, I thought they were going to kill me, and I kept asking for the guards to help me. A psychiatrist saw me.

She was crude at first. Like I was trying to get drugs. I finally said, 'Look! They are going to kill me!' I looked at her and saw something like pity on her face. She had me put on suicidal watch. Believe me, I was glad to be alone!"

"How did you get from jail to here?" I was curious to know.

"I don't know! I haven't talked to Donna yet. Somehow I had a lawyer, and somehow I ended up here. Believe me, this may be a crazy house, but it is far better than jail!"

I looked down at the cuts on my arms, now healed. What could have been so bad? My memory of the last year was sketchy, at best.

We sat for a while in silence, and then I started telling a story. "There was a program in the 1950's called "Queen for a Day." Three women contestants would describe their hardships and dire circumstances. They would cry and bemoan their lives, and it was pathetic. But this was a sick, sick program, looking back on it.

At the end of the morose program, each woman would get a round of applause. An "applause meter", much like the clocks around here, would measure the intensity of their suffering with a needle that moved like a pointed second hand clockwise from one on the left (not very sad) to a ten on the right (tragic). The woman with the highest recorded applause would be crowned, robed, and designated as Queen for the Day. She would be given whatever she needed to ease her suffering—washing machines, screw drivers, pots and pans—whatever was needed to ease the woman's suffering.

One woman had the most pitiful story I had ever heard. Her husband had lost his leg in World War II. He would sit in his favorite arm chair and drink beer every day until by evening he was drunk and belching. One evening he got so drunk he blew his head off. 'And he's still sitting there in his favorite chair 'cuz we can't afford a casket.' She started crying and wailing, and many in the audience joined her, dabbling their eyes and blowing their nose.

Naturally, this woman's story went well into the tragic range, far above the other two contestants. She was robbed and crowned, an ornate metal casket was rolled down the aisle of the studio audience. She was …uh…Queen for the Day."

Martha looked at me incredulously. "Did you make that up?"

I cracked with laughter and said, "Not the program, but the casket part."

She started holding her hands around her waist, laughing maniacally, with tears rolling down her face. "You are CRAZY!"

"Certified."

I laughed, too, uncontrollably. It occurred to me that I had not laughed since being in the "lunatic asylum."

Martha lit up another cigarette. The laughter had stopped and she had that glazed look in her eyes again, perhaps the cigarette took her far away.

"Thank you," I said in a quiet voice.

"What? You wanna' cigarette?"

"Nope. Don't smoke. Thanks for helping me feel alive."

War Bird

I have
been a-witching and
wheeling in
flight!

Free of
body and soul
I am
a nocturnal spirit
exhilarated!

Fly high,
bird of
my own creation,

Dive
sear
soar,

stab with
your beak
the wine- colored stones that
are the eyes of the deer

And screech,
Bird,
Screech,
"I,
I am the Victor!"

Chapter Eight

War Bird

Each morning we met at 10:00 in the conference room on B2. The group discussed a variety of topics, and Dr. Houser made it understood that he was one of an elect few trained in psychoanalysis. He tried to teach his Freudian hypothecations, but was often met with resistance and outright ridicule. Here was a group of women who he was trying to teach were "castrating females." Most of us had been subject to sexual abuse, verbal abuse or physical abuse at the hands of MEN, and it was both amusing and inspiring to seeing these women stand up and say, in effect, "Look, damnit, I was the victim!"

One woman really put Freud in the pot. Dr. Houser was teaching about the Freudian concept of penis envy. "Women," he said, "grow up resenting males for their penis. When they realize they cannot acquire one, they begin, subconsciously to castrate males. It is called, 'penis envy.'"

"Penis envy? Penis envy?" One woman immediately both questioned and confronted this concept. "Are you for real? I don't want one of those things! Why would I want one of them things, all hanging down?"

The group broke up into hysterical laughter. Order was forgotten for more than a several minutes. The women were talking and laughing among themselves. I knew he thought himself quite an expert on bringing out the hidden secrets of mentally sick patients, but he was a little too quick to expose his own sicknesses, though not necessarily intentionally.

Well, I remember a day when he was talking that my stomach went from queasiness to the desire to vomit. The topic was valid enough. We were discussing how we did not have to act on our feelings. He began one of his personal examples.

"Yesterday, I had my adopted son in my lap. I was playing with him, and I began to get a 'little erection.' I knew I was going to do nothing about it. So, I continued holding him."

Inappropriate, I thought. Undoubtedly, some of these women had children. What were they thinking? It was obvious looking at the silent group. They were looking down at their hands, fiddling with their rings or watches. What the hell is a 'little erection' anyway? Maybe he had penis envy. I knew if I was a psychiatrist and had this experience, I would not be sharing it with a group of women I was facilitating.

He was a controversial character, at the least. I once was discussing my obsession with death. I said I could not rid myself of the desire to kill myself. It seemed if we were going to die, anyway, why would we continue in this agony over the fact we were going to die?

"Either shit or get off the pot," was his reply to this plea for some answer, some reason to continue to exist.

I said nothing, but replied mentally, *Yes. At the right moment, so I will do*

My final day in group was the day my social worker appeared in the middle of our session. She did not announce why she was there, or even introduce herself to the group, but sat quietly in a vacant chair. After she sat and observed for about fifteen minutes, she announced. "I am here to talk about Lynn's discharge. We have a summer job for her, and she will be going back to University of Louisville in the fall. She will be staying at Colonial Inn, our half-way house for women."

Though after leaving the state hospital I did not immediately break communication with him, I eventually moved away from all ties to Dr. Houser. I read years and years later he had been convicted of drug related charges. The article I read did not go into details.

As far as leaving the hospital, I suppose it was natural to feel both excitement and dread. I knew had an appointment to keep, pushed by the reckless statement of Dr. Houser, but yet the thought of walking down the sidewalk, going to class, a job, triggered a buried feeling-excitement.

I did not look behind as my social worker and I left the hospital. My thoughts were directed at starting a new job. It was my first job! I so badly wanted to be a good worker. I had been told I would be sorting camera film in a processing company. About 12 students had been hired to do the work for the summer rush.

I had not visited the half-way house either. I only knew there were seven other women there at the time, and another woman, besides myself, was expected to be there in a couple of weeks. I did not know how the house was run, but I did not have to pay rent. I could put aside my money for school in the fall.

I had called my father to tell him I was being discharged, but he seemed distant and disinterested. It did not disappoint me. I had developed attachments outside of my family and outside of the life I had known, and to a large extent, could not remember. My mother would come to mind, and I would be overcome with guilt and sadness. I dismissed her quickly from my mind whenever those thoughts surged like a storm.

I entered Colonial Inn from the front door. It was an old house in a historic area of town, easily acceptable to the downtown area where I would work that summer. Facing me was a stairway, leading up to the bedrooms, where each resident shared a room with one or more other residents. I, at once, noticed the quiet in the house. The other residents had not returned home. Each was expected to work, attend school, or be earnestly looking for work.

The woman who ran the house came to meet me. She, from her tone of voice and warmth she exhibited, seemed like a kind, caring soul. She introduced herself, and the social worker who had brought me excused herself and left.

"I am Cherrish," she said, taking one of my bags. "My husband is upstairs. He helps me direct the activities of the house. First, let me show you to your room, and then I will explain the house policies."

A toddler, who had been hiding, unseen by me, behind a door in the hallway, made his way to his mother. He tentatively sized me up, his finger hanging languidly from his mouth.

"Hi, there! What's your name?" I greeted him, but he hid his face in his mother clothes.

"This is Marcus," his mother answered for him. "He will get to know you in time, though I must admit, he's very much a 'mama's boy.'"

My room was quite comfortable, especially compared to that which I had become comfortable. There was a desk and an armchair, and the hardwood floor was covered with a well-worn rug that had faded to a brownish gold. I imagined myself writing poetry and sitting at the desk typing the poems to perfection. It was a good, wholesome feeling, a feeling of anticipation of finding ways to accomplish, to establish myself once again as a student. I had written a lot of poetry during my hospitalizations, and I was determined to find some way of getting them read by someone who would appreciate them.

After I finished unpacking, I went down the stairs to meet with Cherrish. I walked quietly, like the stillness of the house was something sacred I was not to break. I was unsure that I would, indeed, make it back into the community, that I would falter at some point and fail at school or my summer job.

Cherrish and I talked, and she explained the women took turns cooking supper, cleaning up after the meal, and cleaning the house once a week. Each woman must always clean up after herself—dishes were not to be left in the sink. One evening in the week we had a meeting all were to attend. We decided as a group which chores each would do and planned the menus for the coming week. Groceries and household supplies would be provided.

As we finished our talk, the women began trickling in from their daily activities. Six months was the usual stay, although several women came and went while I was there. There was Rose, who was the devout Christian of the group. Her eyes had sadness, and her Christianity did not appeal to me because of a certain martyrdom that accompanied it. In ways she was a wonderful person who without complaining would reach out to help when a woman was in need—all too often at her own expense. This quality, I learned much later was a little too close to my own conception of Christianity with which I had struggled since childhood.

There was Kathleen, who seemed to exist in another dimension. She came from a poor family, and her goal was to go to "charm school" to learn how to be a lady with perfect manners. She carried cloth handkerchief, which she would drop at the feet of men, hoping one would retrieve it for her and become her Beloved.

Diane, an African American woman, was quite adept at sizing up a situation. She was very gentle, though. Just, of all of us, probably saw reality more clearly. She stuttered terribly in those days, which made conversation difficult.

To be honest, I do not remember the others. But, how well I remember the expected woman who came in one afternoon after I had but been at Colonial Inn but a couple of weeks. It was Martha! I was so delighted to see her! She looked at me and started laughing, that laughter of total lack of self-consciousness.

Her social worker and her former roommate Donna were with her. Donna was pregnant. It was obvious. But, looking at the two of them, I saw two people that invited me to know them as they were.

"Hi! It's me!" Martha greeted me.

"It would be very odd if you were someone other than you!"

"They let me out of the crazy house! Can you believe it?"

"I can't believe you are here. I am so glad to see you!"

Cherrish took her to her room and then gave her the rap. We all sat at the table and ate together, and what was to be a tumultuous adventure began. The first night Martha and I were reunited I took her to have a Coke at a little restaurant that was a couple of blocks away. Martha was going to be looking for a job. She had a good work record, and it did not take her long to find employment.

Donna became a frequent visitor there, often sharing dinner at our table. I very soon learned her life was extremely difficult at the time, with financial difficulties and struggling with the prospect of a baby.

Somehow I retrieved my typewriter from my father's house, and I began compulsively working at writing my poetry. I was also working at my summer job which put me in a very healthy environment in the community. I packed my lunch each day, and the other teenagers and I hired for the summer would all sit in a shaded area and talk about everything from religion to the current folk singers which marked the era in which we were living.

Donna knew a lot of Christians in the community. She invited us to a charismatic group that met in the basement of a building which I do not know was a church or a bank or a funeral home. But, there was glorious singing and praising the Lord. At first, I was very impressed, until the minister said, "We need to get some business men and such in here. People to add some stability." This was the first red flag. I wanted to believe the suffering, the poor, the sinners were of the first importance. The church gradually drifted into a kind of hierarchal power system, making me question their claim, as the professed in song that we were "One in the Spirit." The system worked like a pyramid sales approach. We were taught to "serve upward." This was against, completely, against my views of Christianity and all religions. The most important, to me, especially after the suffering I had seen, were the ones who were not the "pretty people." Leadership from the top began to be sternly enforced.

I was interested though, very deeply, in this group, though I had some very serious questions about their ideology. My depressions were taking root again, and with them the obsession with suicide and death. I remembered Dr. Houser, and the promise I had made to myself, my appointment with infinity, with Dr. Houser's statement. I needed help from somewhere—at first it seemed I would find it from this charismatic group.

One family I met there became life-long friends. Their generosity and entirely sincere searching for the meaning of being a Christian was and is obvious. Lynda, a very kind, merciful person took those of us associated with Colonial Inn as her family. Social status was not important to her. If she saw a need, she did her best to serve God by meeting that need. There were others, also, that sought a more pure, fulfilling path to true peace than was offered in the traditional churches.

Lynda was a friend to us. Not a pedagogue. Something she showed us about ourselves was that we need not define ourselves by the illnesses that had brought us together, to the Colonial inn. Martha and I, especially, when introduced to people would in short order say, "We're from Central State." We would look down in shame.

Lynda confronted this. "Why do you do that? Why do you say you are from Central State? You talk as though you were born and raised there!"

We thought this quite funny, but, oh the truth in that statement. The stigma of mental illness, still today present, makes people with a psychiatric diagnosis define themselves as such. The stigma can be as consuming as the illness itself.

Not too long after I had started going to the Christian gathering, frocked for me in disillusionment, I started talking about suicide. People often have the misconception that if a person says they will kill themselves, they will not. They are simply seeking attention. What does that mean, "seeking attention?" If it means, "I have this dreadful drive to end this crazy life, and I am wavering literally between life and death," then yes, I suppose the individual is crying out to God and other people that the agony is almost greater than they can bear. Would a person with a ruptured appendix cry out, "Hey! Something is very, very wrong! I need help!"? Would this be a plea for attention? I, personally, having experienced the seemingly unending deliberation of the value of my life, have taken each person with whom I have been in contact who even hints at the indication they are in that place very, very seriously. It is time at that point for intervention.

But, I had been told to "shit or get off the pot." I went to a place of hiding and swallowed a whole bottle of Thorazine that Dr. Houser had given me. I was found semi-conscious, but was a terrifying, horrendous experience. I don't remember being treated in the ER. I remember my pounding heart and an awareness of that even though unconscious. After I recovered physically, Dr. Houser insisted I return to Colonial Inn. The experience did one thing—the horror of it prevented returned me from trying this again for about a decade. The basic problem was yet to be resolved. I read a book, *A Man's Search for Meaning*, by Victor Frankel. It described how people, including himself, who had meaning in their lives, survived in concentration camps in World War II at a far higher percentage than those who had no reason to survive. When he returned from the concentration camp, he, a psychiatrist, developed a form of therapy called "logotherapy," which helped suffering people find meaning to move away from their suffering into a fuller life. My meaning became my search for meaning.

I became involved in school work, and it was a diversion, to an extent, from questioning the validity of any belief that would give "meaning" to a life full of pain and suffering. Particularly, the writing of my poetry was a diversion from the constant hammering of existential angst. I was taking another creative writing class, and I would slide my poems under the professor's door. I wrote with my Heart. I wrote of my pain. I sometimes wrote of beauty, but even beauty is fleeting. Even pleasure eventually brings pain.

One day I came back from school, and there was a message from my professor. I was to call him. Uncertain of what he could possibly want, I was afraid to call. But, I dialed the number and to my surprise was offered a scholarship in Creative Writing. This was what I needed to bring me from the scourge of hell. It gave me confidence as a writer, and I began writing with even more intensity. It was Dr. Harvey Webster, my professor who procured the scholarship for me from the English Department. A glowing letter soon came, documenting the award.

Martha and I celebrated with a Coke from our restaurant. Martha and I dealt with issues that were the same in many ways. Although my angst and despair now expressed itself in hysterical crying or withdrawal to bed, Martha would become angry and lash out—many times at me because we were close friends.

But, we muddled along as people do in life. Acceptance of each other was so important in a house of people with psychiatric issues. Slowly, though, we came out of hiding.

Cherrish's husband, however, was showing signs of deterioration. Cherrish would say things like, "Never marry a man who won't work." It became obvious we, the residents, were not alone in having serious issues.

We would see him hiding behind doorways, watching. He started telling me he knew what I was doing. I was trying to make him sick. He said he knew I would leave the room whenever he came in. I was aghast at this accusation because if I had been doing that I certainly wasn't aware of it. But, he was removed from logic.

One day the couple announced they were leaving and would appreciate it if we left Colonial Inn as soon as possible. We were confused and at a loss as where to go or how we would manage. No preparation had been given.

But, admirably, we rallied together. We moved across the street into three or four apartments in the same building. We decided we would stick together and somehow get through this. It was an opening of a door, a closer life to the life of the community at large.

Both Martha and I had moved away from the charismatic church. We began acting erratically. The two of us could become quite exuberant, verging on outright mania or our frustration and feelings of inadequacy would make us enemies for a time. I remember one time for some reason I had my father's Jeep (I cannot remember how much contact I had with him), but I did not have a driver's license. Martha and I went for a joy ride, but not down the streets; we went down the sidewalks. We were laughing and howling maniacally, and I, an untrained driver, was swerving to the left or to the right. Neither of us used even alcohol at that point in our lives. But, sometimes it was as if we were out of our minds ....mania?

I remember that Christmas mother had sent me, unexpectedly, a box of clothes. I had received them and was opening them with kind of a dismal mixture of guilt and appreciation. Martha walked in with a plate of food for me. Seeing the lavish gifts, she threw the plate against the wall. The plate in slow motion slid down the white wall, leaving a green and brown trail of peas and pork behind it. It was actually rather funny, looking back, but the two of us took ourselves very seriously. I was self-righteously hurt, and she was furious that I should get such attention from a family member. (Why the hell did I get these lavish gifts, and she got none?)

The experiment in supportive living came to an end one evening when our landlady appeared. She came to evict us. It seems she had decided that she had figured out we were prostitutes, and Rose was the Madam. This threw Martha into a fit of laughter. "Rose doesn't even date!" she proclaimed to the person. But, she wanted us out that night, or she was calling the police.

We left. But we took all the light bulbs and any fixtures we could. The place was barren. We were full of merriment, even though the group was unsure where to go or how we would manage.

Martha and I remained friends, and Rose tried to stay in contact with all of us. But it was the end of a chapter from a saga that smacks, once again, of absurdity.

I honestly cannot remember where I went from there. I remember Martha helping me out when I was hospitalized and had surgery to have my gallbladder removed. Martha, after the surgery, arranged for me to recuperate at Lynda and Sidney's home.

It was there I got the news of my mother's illness. I got a phone call with no knowledge that my mother was sick that she had her lung removed for lung cancer. Martha and Lynda were there. I was doubled over in deep pain and tears. Sobs and wails from me filled the house. Were it not for these friends, I would have had to bear the pain alone.

Lynda, Martha, and I drove to Owensboro, KY to visit my mother, with her oxygen, various tubes, and all the artifacts of a hospital room. We talked to her, though she could barely speak. Lynda made her laugh by telling her she had received more "points" for her surgery than I could ever cash in for mine.

I could not allow myself to think of the possible outcomes of this surgery. When I talked to her doctor, I found him infuriating.

"We don't know if the cancer will come back, but we just go on from here," he said, rather matter-of-factly.

I was immediately angered. "Of course the cancer won't come back!" I thought to myself. "Why is he even suggesting that it will?"

It seemed so inconceivable that a forty-six-year-old woman could die! No! I would NOT go there! But, in the months ahead, the doubts would break through the denial. The possibility, even the likelihood, was there. The doctor had said the tumor was as large as a grapefruit. Impossible! (People died at all ages, came to my mind. I could die at any time.)

After my mother had recovered from the surgery, I made the decision to visit her in my home town. Martha had left for California, to be with an old boyfriend. I loathed going, but felt it was time I faced the reality I had a mother with whom I needed to make peace.

I think I drove down to see Mother in the old Jeep. I drove past the church that was so much a part of my life in my early youth. I looked at the long flight of wide concrete steps leading to the door of the sanctuary. Did my faith fail me, or did I fail my faith? Perhaps the activities in which I was engaged when I started my descent into a world where there was no meaning, no Light, were not really as Evil as I thought. Even if I did veer from the way, so to speak, how easy to ask for forgiveness. But, to be truly forgiven, I believed, one must have the intention of laying down the divisive sword which splits into the conscience. I didn't know at this point. What I know, by now, I would never be able to live in peace without the Light of God. For me, each time I denied that Light, I brought upon myself pain and suffering. Each time, though difficult, I chose the path that was the most difficult, but, in my mind the most loving, compassionate, way, I experienced grace. In the long run it was the easier path. I would with time discard the useless remnants of superstition, based largely on fear, embrace new ideologies, but, at the same time, not deny the faith that had as much embraced me as I had embraced it.

"I cannot help it because I am mentally ill," for me was not acceptable, and never would be. I may not be able to stop the winds of my moods and confusion, but I must take responsible actions to make my life better. Thinking like this, as I drove down Main Street, I felt a glimmer of hope. If only I could follow through and be an integrated self, compassionate to myself, and, in turn, compassionate towards others. I was not ready yet to accept this as an Unfailing Truth in the path to recovery.

The sight of my old home, the sight of my mother standing in the doorway, brought fear, insecurity, and a desire to turn around and drive away. Was it a feeling of "ought to" that brought me here or a true love for the woman who brought me into the world? Most things take the perspective of time to see with clarity. The turbid emotions I felt were not brought on by my choice. At this point I *was* a victim. *At what point could I choose to be otherwise?*

My mother was excited to see me it seemed. There was not hesitancy in either of our expression of a greeting. But, there was no hug, for that was something not established in our family. What was going on in her thinking? Was she fearful, as I was that the cancer would return? Did she blame me, as I blamed her, for the unhappiness in her life? It was such a disgrace to the family that no one was told about my psychiatric hospitalization, though I suspected some knew. Maybe many knew.

We talked about school and my scholarship. We talked about my grandfather, who had died during my hospitalization. We talked about my sister and her husband and child.

But, we did not talk about the emotional issues that separated our family members from each other, a split like a tree hit with an ax. You stood on your side of the tree and did not cross the ground between.

My mother had always been good at triggering guilt, however, and she took an opportunity to jab me with that knife. She said, "You don't know how you made me suffer." It was me. I was the cause. I probably even caused the cancer! The handful of my hair in her hand as she beat me, it was me. I heard, but this time I understood. I looked at her without revealing my disdain for her cowardliness. She had yet to face herself. To see. To really see.

I went in my room to see my precious collection of angels. But, they were gone.

I came out and said, "My angels!"

"Oh, Lynn," she dismissed me, "they collected dust."

"Yes, yes," I said sarcastically, but to myself, not her, "they collected dust. *Did they make you angry? Sad? What was your real motive in getting rid of them? Did you throw them and break them?*"

I stayed one night and left. I felt the need to get away as soon as possible. This house was haunted. Haunted with the memories of abuse and emotional violence. I left relieved. Whatever my life in Louisville, in spite of the depression and despair, there was at least hope of finding my own way.

The next time I went to see her was in the spring. It was obvious something was terribly wrong. I stayed as long as I could bear to, but I knew I could not be the one to care for her. She was racked with pain in her spine. She had become terribly thin. I was terrified. In spite of any sort of secret loathing, I could not tolerate thinking she would die.

My mother would not let me call my older sister to help because she had just had her second child. They gave her one radiation treatment in Owensboro to "help with the pain."

"They said my spine was fractured," she explained to me.

"How did your spine get fractured?"

"Compression."

"Compression from what?" I persisted.

She shrugged and answered, "Just compression."

I drove to my grandmother and said I could not take care of my mother. She called my sister in New Jersey, who came the next day with the second child. I left to return to the dorm room in which I had taken residence and registered for school.

My sister called me the following weekend. "You better get home. She doesn't have long." "Okay. I'll come next weekend."

"You better come today."

I left for "home," dreading what I would see, and dreading even more what I would feel. It was worse than I could have imagined. Pain management then was not nearly as advanced as it is now.

Although the obsessive fear of death I had almost took my life, so young, the fear of seeing my mother, staring Death in the eyes, afraid like a child, was not even something I could admit I was witnessing, not in reality, not in her mind or mine. We had to lie, up to the bitter end.

Marriage

our marriage
was the marriage of
the pine to the forest
rich smell of the woods
and its wildflowers
ferns and clear streams

I climbed your
damp haunches
and smoothed my
face against your
rough bark

early though
we drank from
different cups
cups in fact that
were never merged
into one chalice

we experienced the
change in season

the winter brought us
isolation in different
homes no longer sharing laughter
no longer giving
gentle looks
different dreams at night
We had drunk the red wine of marriage
and birthing but had lived to see
the death of what was gained

Chapter Nine

Marriage

I grieved for many years for my mother. My sister and I would talk of the violence and tensions in our home as we grew up. Still, there is a bond between mother and daughter that goes beyond any of the horrors that may have occurred in the past. I still grieve for her, but not for her death. I grieve for her life. It was as though her heart was in a glass jar with a sealed lid. She could not let the love in because she could not let the love out. I am only speculating, but I believe it was pain and what she saw as the insignificance of her own life and a disconnection between her and her family and friends that caused the violent outbursts. Perhaps there was a mental illness from which she suffered, also. It took decades of examining, re-examining the relationship between us to see that she probably was not even aware of that glass jar, and furthermore, had she recognized it, had no idea how to break through it. This is the interpretation of her life to which I have come. Maybe I am entirely wrong. I will never know for honest communication never really occurred, as, fortunately, it has with my daughter and me. It saddens me to think of all she sacrificed to keep that glass shell from even showing a splinter of a crack.

Different people reacted sometimes in odd ways to my grief, I remember. I returned from the funeral to my dorm room. My roommate, who I had only met the week before, reacted so peculiarly it brought a rolling laughter, involuntarily, from me.

"What did you do when you left this weekend?" she asked upon my return.

"Well, my mother died. I went to the funeral."

"Oh," she said and paused, looked obviously disconcerted, and then she added, quietly. "Well, I hope it wasn't anything serious."

I never got to know this young woman well, but suspected she personally had yet to experience anything that affected one so intensely. She certainly knew little about me, either. The distance between us pushed me to find another roommate.

During the intense part of my grieving, there were many nightmares. I would dream dreams I cannot bear to even describe, for the horrors in them were unimaginable, much worse than the events that led to them. The reality of our lives as mother and daughter is tragic enough. I would bolt up in the middle of an indescribable scene between my mother, her corpse, and myself. A psychologist suggested I could control the dreams, tell her to go back to wherever it was she was supposed to be. I was, in fact, able to become aware in my sleep that I was dreaming and determine the outcome of the dream. I practiced each night before sleep.

I also exhibited behaviors that are now a source of regret for me. I understand it now. I do not feel guilt for I have acceptance forgiveness from God and my own conscience, but I regret that they occurred.

For one thing, I had never stolen to my memory. For about six months I engaged in shoplifting. They would be senseless acts. I remember buying a whole shopping cart of groceries and paying for them, but putting a can of tuna in my purse. I took risks that would have brought criminal charges. I do not understand the dynamics of this behavior, but I know it had to do with the grieving process. Then, one day, six months later, I said to myself, "I don't have to do this anymore." And I completely stopped, never to return to this behavior again.

The other way I put myself in danger was through allowing sexual exploitation. What particularly comes to mind is a situation in which I repeatedly put myself. There was a guy, who seemed to have no soul. He was devoid of expression. I don't know how this started, but at first after mother died I was a zombie. I walked, dazed, confused. I would walk out of the dorm, and he would be there.

He would take me to his car, and every time this walk led to me having oral sex with him. I despised it. I despised myself. I would pray that God would help me through it—get it over with. He would lead me through the act, and let it be known that once I "turned him on" and it was my responsibility to "finish." It was revolting, nauseating, and I blamed myself, only.

These were acts of hatred towards myself, violating any sort of moral code I had. Even though my faith was faltering, I felt that a true spiritual quest was what my Heart of hearts craved. I denied it, though. I could not accept the rigid limits of the Church, but was uncomfortable with the sexual freedom movement of the sixties. I did not have established within my own conscience a clear set of values by which I could live.

I got involved with a graduate student who taught Freshmen English. He had played basketball for U of L, was commissioned as an officer in the war in Viet Nam, and came back a long haired pot smoking hippie with a moustache. He was clearly a good guy, though somewhat abrupt. A marriage between us would never have worked, but he and I had some good times together. I was still grieving my mother, and was often sullen and withdrawn. He would confront me on issues, but I still was unable to defend my position. To stand up to a man would be something I would have to learn in years ahead. I wrote poetry, which he encouraged. He introduced me to James Taylor, who became my favorite musical artist.

We two flower children of the sixties went on a road trip to California, traveling on the way there through the Southwestern states. It was June, and the weather was gentle with us. We had a pup tent, a hibachi, a cooler full of food, maps, and lots and lots of pot. We visited cities and countryside alike. We pitched our tent as we traveled toward LA, whenever the sun became low in the sky and we were ready to eat. We visited the Grand Canyon, stayed in a casino hotel in Las Vegas, and, indeed I loved the ride.

We visited Martha and her husband in LA, and several of us went to Tijuana for a day's sojourn for cheap souvenirs and the experience of being in Mexico. Martha had a pill loose in her purse, and we were detained at the border on our way back into the US. I could see, but not hear, Martha arguing with the authorities. I thought, "Oh, my God! Jailed, returning from Mexico!" I never knew how it was decided we could re-enter. But, we made it back, and spent the evening with our grass and wine coolers. Safe in the US.

On the day we left it was warm and sunny in LA, and we arrived to a cool, rainy San Francisco at the home of a couple that were friends of my sister. Going into San Francisco, I was frightened by the hills. It was a roller coaster ride on narrow slick roads, but the ambience was clearly one of freedom from the Establishment. I felt that I was in the heart of all the beliefs for which our radical friends stood. It of tasted of liberation and rebellion, as we saw it then. A rush of feeling, a connection with all that stood for Peace, and the "Age of Aquarius." It was like a strong gust of continuous wind, filling me with desire for more liberation from the torment of mixed beliefs.

Quite different was our next visit in the West. We were at Lake Tahoe, the two of us in total isolation. Pulling in late, we pitched our tent. The ground was miserably cold and hard. As I slept that night in my sleeping bag on the floorless ground of the tent, I grew more and more cold. It became a numbing cold.

Morning came, and I opened the flaps of the tent. My companion was standing next to a flaming pile of wood. Though the fire was appealing and the mountain was glorious as the sun reflected off the cover of snow on the boughs of the giant evergreens, I wanted only to get into the warm car and flee down the mountain. We always left the campsite before breakfast, but here, with two feet of snow everywhere, this crazy guy wants to eat breakfast. It seemed insane and I was aggravated.

However, with the sense of duty that only a woman knows, I prepared on the open fire the bacon, the eggs, and the biscuits. As the fire warmed me and the food filled my stomach, I looked at the peace around me. This was not the peace demanded by protest; it was the peace of surrender, of letting go of the perceptions of injustice in my life. Does a tree feel injustice as snow weighs heavily on its branches? Is there injustice or justice in this real world? All beings suffer. There is no discrimination. Seasons come of pleasure, moments like now when the Earth seems like the garden it is, replenishing itself season after season. Likewise, come the seasons of pain. Do we shake our fists at the Heavens because of the change from summer to winter? This does not release me from my desire to somehow touch and relieve the pain of one, just one hurting spirit. It only intensified and reminded me of what I still could not grasp—the responsibility to oneself to intend no harm—every living thing is fighting a very hard battle. Every living thing is reaching for the Light. Swimming upward. Looking for the warmth of the fire. For a moment I felt a sense of purpose, a call for compassion. But, I had yet to realize that life does not just heap things upon us—we have choices—always choices.

As we packed to leave the site, I took one last look at the snow. It would be a long time before the season would return.

The rest of our route home seemed like endless driving. St. Louis, the Gateway to the West.

"I knew that Lake Tahoe would be our last real stop," my friend commented as we went through the arches. "That is why I wanted to have breakfast at Lake Tahoe."

When we returned home, I was told he had another girlfriend. He was honest with me, but my old friend, denial, hung around for some months after. The night he told me, he played James Taylor for me, singing, "Hey, ain't it good to know that you got a friend ..." One more relationship. More nights alone.

I walked the university grounds and saw some people sitting on the lawn beside the library. There were long haired men and women, the friends to whom I was attracted. I sat and listened to the conversations. They centered around political issues. I noticed a certain cynicism, a spirit of rebellion, and a variance from the norm. This appealed to me. I was looking for answers. Maybe these people knew something I should learn.

As the days passed, I became interested in a very unusual man with a long, dark ponytail. Before I knew it, I was at his home in a very poor neighborhood. He vowed he was a communist and was dedicated to overthrowing the government and giving the power to the working class. Though I thought of those whose spiritual beliefs had been suppressed by communism, the politics he described intrigued me.

It wasn't long before I was smoking pot with him and his group of friends and became sexually involved with him. We would get stoned and watched Marx Brother and Woody Allen movies. Frankly, with the dope in me I could never begin to understand what was going on in the movies. His music did not appeal to me—hard rock. He had a Jewish background, though until much later in life, he showed no real interest in what this meant to him except for the food his family and their friends would enjoy. Often, we went to an authentic Jewish deli and had kosher corn beef on rye. There were many aspects of the culture he would describe, but the importance to him in his personal life appeared much later in his life. He followed certain traditions to honor his parents, and this impressed me as authentic.

I would sometimes wonder about the wisdom of being involved with someone who came from a completely different sociological background than I. I did not see it as a really insurmountable problem, though I did not feel the freedom to follow in the pursuit of God, as I saw Him. It was not that this freedom was denied me by him; it was that the dilemma was ever present. *What did I believe?*

Unlike the other relationships I had with men, this one seemed to deepen, instead of grow apart—at first. I grew to love him and respected his intelligence and appreciated his rather odd sense of humor. We had shared moments where we told our secret longings and aspirations. Neither of us, however, seemed to have a sense of the future or an idea of what we wanted to accomplish with our lives or what it meant to be committed to one another.

"Why don't we get married?" I asked one day.

Gabriel, as was his name, was married at the time. It would have necessitated a divorce, although he had minimal contact with his wife. He had become a heroin addict in New York City. His mother, who was a Hungarian woman, a very strong mother and wife, had gone to him, sick in the hospital with hepatitis, and offered him a car and financial support if he would leave New York and come to Louisville to go to school. It is to his credit that he never went back to the drug and did earnestly seek a degree at U of L.

It was not to my credit that I became involved with someone who was married, no matter how estranged they were. It was not to my credit, either, that we married without him yet resolving the issue of the importance of such a commitment.

I remember when he agreed to marriage, although I do not remember insisting upon the engagement. I was in the dining area, sitting at the table working on an assignment. What he said to me was exciting but also disappointing to me. "Lynn, if you think we ought to get married, I think we should."

His ambivalence on issues often confused me. It was less than a mutual desire, even less than a compromise. It was a giving in. It was, instead of a commitment that brought me joy, an agreement by him that brought me guilt. I bore much guilt throughout the relationship. That was often undeserved.

We did get married, and had an unusual ceremony that was representative of the unusual bond between us. The rehearsal dinner was humorous and reflected the differences between our cultural backgrounds. My father arranged it at one of the most expensive restaurants in town. The two families sat and ate together, one family at one end and one at the other. Each father would lean over and say a disparaging comment about the other family. My future mother-in-law kept screaming at the servers in her thick Hungarian accent, "More bread! We need more bread at the table! Darling, where is our bread?" Our choice of restaurants was unacceptable to them, and my family, my father and stepmother, made comments within the hearing range of all at the table about how uncouth this family was. Gabriel, our friends, and I were all drunk and found this a hilarious scene—perhaps one that should be in one of those movies we watched. I thought it was funny, but at the same time I also found it embarrassing. I was embarrassed for the players in this comedy.

The wedding went more smoothly. I was in a satin bell bottomed pant suit with tiny pink flowers, carrying cascading pink roses. Gabriel was in a suit we had picked out. My sister, eight months pregnant with her third child, wore a flowing pink gown. We all had a great time. Gabriel's brother, who was his best man, kept leaning towards me saying such funny things I could hardly say my vows. It is obvious in the wedding pictures that I was shaking with laughter.

When we boarded on the plane for our honeymoon at my in-law's condominium on Miami Beach and plans for Disney World, a flight attendant asked if we were newlyweds. When we acknowledged this, they offered us champagne. No chance of that happening today.

We drove from Miami Beach to Disney World, and I was reminded of that blue glass ball, full of memories of happy endings to fairy tales. Full, also, of lies and delusional thinking—delusional in the sense that some "gain" in the world was a source of happiness. You marry a prince, and you live happily ever after. I put on my rose colored glasses and believed for a moment in the truth of childhood fantasies.

Our honeymoon was magical for the moment. Would it stand the test of a change of focus, of establishing a home life that had a concrete foundation? A psychiatrist told me years later that to have a good relationship you have to be willing to "kiss a lot of ass." In my immaturity, I saw a relationship as something that would meet MY needs. I had learned of pain and suffering, but thought somehow those dissolved when you "built your own life." I had felt true suffering, but did not know how to deal with building an emotionally, spiritually, and financially secure home.

Early on we fought about my instability in maintaining employment. I worked as a substitute teacher, and Gabriel got a job at the State Hospital as a social worker. I don't know why young women think this, but many women do, and I, too, felt a baby would bring us closer. I did not understand the responsibility of birthing a child. I wanted a baby. I was not solid in my role in the relationship, and I do not think Gabriel was either. At first he thought it was something, again saying since I wanted it, we should do. I was using the rhythm method of birth control, afraid of taking "the pill" with all the side effects. Then he changed his mind. He said was not ready. I did initiate sex in the middle of my fertility period. He did not take responsibility for his part in the act. In fact, he said to me, "Bitch!"

It did not take long for the morning sickness to hit. Gabriel said, "Well, I guess you are pregnant." Such disgust for me.

Yet, when the pregnancy test was positive, he did not hesitate for a moment to call his parents and tell them. We bought a house with the help of his family. We went to natural childbirth classes. Gabriel seemed content, but, I was afraid to ask how he really felt.

Still, I did not have a steady job. During my pregnancy I secured an educational loan and went to graduate school to get certified as a high school librarian. It was a goal-oriented project that drained me during the last months of my pregnancy, but I completed it. I completed the field work after the baby was born.

When I saw the bond was irrevocably broken, however, was after the precious girl was born, and Gabriel had his friend from work, Martin, move in with us. I was so, so tired and depressed. I was not interested in sex. All I wanted was one long uninterrupted night asleep. Almost the entire care of the child was mine. And the house. And the cooking. Once a dead animal was in the driveway and Gabriel's response was, "You want to be the homemaker, you get rid of the thing." My friend Lynda and her husband came over when Gabriel left to help rid me of the carcass.

Martin and Gabriel would laugh and talk late at night. I remember when I witnessed the unthinkable happening. I took the baby and drove in the night around and around the city, thinking. Having no other option, I returned home.

From there, it is a splintered story. I found a job. But the next year, when the teachers were near a strike for better working conditions and pay, I, a first year teacher, got laid off. Gabriel left. I, who had suffered deep depression after the birth of the child, sank further into despair. I ended up in a psychiatric hospital for a month. It was the beginning of a new decade in my life. A decade of losing all hope of ever finding that fairy tale ending. Hospitalizations. Suicide attempts. A gut level searching for a reason to continue. For her sake, I gave beloved child to my now ex-husband to raise. It was the beginning of over a decade of self-destruction.

on losing my child

the prehistoric bird caws

> *her screech confined*
> *to the walls of her skull*

unspeakable is her terror
her torment
when she sees that

> *she has killed her own young*

she wears no wings
but walks the earth and
cries

> *"Have mercy, have mercy."*

Chapter Ten

The Decade of Self-Destruction

The most love I have ever felt was after the birth of my daughter, when they put her in my arms. I never knew it was possible to love so much!

"Look at her hair," I said to Gabriel. She, indeed, had more hair, dark, long, and going in all directions, than any baby in the nursery. Those tiny fingers were perfect! She suckled immediately at my breast.

I will always believe she knew I loved her, even in the womb. The bond for both of us was immediate. I would get calls from the nursery that they needed to bring her to me because she was crying relentlessly. She was comforted as soon as she was in my arms. As a newborn, she always wanted to be with mama.

It was a long labor. Perhaps she didn't want to leave the closeness of the womb. Perhaps I did not want to let go.

My mother-in-law had come to help the day before I came home from the hospital. But, at that point, she thought breastfeeding was "selfish." Twenty years later she told me she thought that then, but had come to believe it was very smart. When my daughter was a newborn, though, her idea of helping was to feed the baby at night. I had caused her to be angry with me. She left after two days.

Gabriel, ironically as the story continues, did not want to show his love for this baby. Obviously, he still resented me. Even in the labor room at one point I saw him looking at me and scowling. It was very deeply painful, more painful than the labor itself. The obstetrician held my hand and gave me ice chips. I felt I deserved no mercy from anyone.

It was obvious from an early age that this child was quite precocious. How quickly she learned that persistent crying got her what she wanted! And how exhausting for me!

It was not the child that caused my postpartum depression, which was un-diagnosed but I was certain it was there. It was caring, basically alone, for the household, the added responsibility, the cooking—there was no one to help. My father was in his own hell, though he did come through at times. My mother was dead and my sister was miles away. I needed a break!

She was quite engaging, my child, as a person. Not only that, but she was truly, objectively beautiful. The mixture of Anglo-Saxon and Eastern European genes gave her an exotic look that was noticed by strangers and friends alike. In the day care she was happy and playful. I put her there when I went to work.

By that time the marriage was crumbling, and very shortly Gabriel left. There was no peace in motherhood. I hoped I could break the chain of abuse that my mother left as her legacy. I felt I was an even worse mother than my worst memories of my mother. I was failing. Instead of disciplining, I was overly permissive. I, in fact, was neglecting my needs. This was, in fact, the failing. Things could have been different had I had someone to take over when I simply was even too exhausted to eat.

I struggled through a school year, and then—only because of my lack of seniority—lost my job. Gabriel stopped paying his child support. I did not re-port him. Finally, my depression was so intense I went to the family doctor and was immediately hospitalized.

The round of repeated hospitalizations had begun. So, too, had the self-inflicted burns and cuts, only they were deep and open wounds, showing the pain that was into my very bone marrow and the crevices of my heart. There was little mercy shown me, but that was okay, for I had no mercy for myself. No one could have hated me as much as I hated myself.

At first, there were times when it seemed I was pulling out of "it." Periods where there were no signs of self-destruction. Hoping to be able once again to care for my daughter, I would work hard to get a job and in time lose the job because of my impairment.

I worked very hard to get a job as a writer for a science and engineering newsletter. I wrote, as a sample of my ability to research and write, an article about the physics of black holes, which was becoming at that time a popular subject. I was told my writing was far superior to any of the other writers who had applied, and I soon was hired.

Before too long, however, I became afraid, terrified of the administrative staff. I actually hid under my desk one day and called Lynda, begging for her to come get me and take me to safety. I began missing work because of fear of the way other staff members were looking at me. One day my symptoms were so severe and my talking so incoherent, the secretary called my doctor and immediately took me to the hospital. Within a week, I was fired.

My mood did not stay in a depressed, anxious state. I would become grandiose and think simple things like the way a paper was lying on a table was a sign God had a special purpose for me. Often, in this state I would visit a church to which I normally would not go. I have been baptized seven times as a Christian. Five of those were in a manic state.

I visited a very large church that is well-established, but somewhat nontraditional. The halogen lights and the smell of the church, like fresh wood, electrified me. I knew something big was going to happen. I felt all that someone had to do to see I was someone special—a great evangelist, or soon to be missionary—was to see the radiant glow around me. I could see it! At the altar call I marched confidently down the aisle to be baptized once again. It would seem they would recognize the purity of my heart as I was raised from the water.

I raced home from this church filled with road rage, angry at all cars that blocked me from speeding down the expressway. "I need clothes," I thought. "Everyone was nicely dressed. To be appreciated, I must have nice clothes. Lord, show me where to get clothes."

I pulled into a mall. Rushing like a fireman, I bought this outfit and that, regardless of the cost. It was the most important thing of my life, enabling these people to see me as a spiritual leader.

I harassed the leaders of this church with calls about the significance of my witnessing to people I met in the grocery, on the street, or people who knew me (who knew something was askew.) Eventually, though, I either fizzled out or was hospitalized. I don't know which was the case in this particular situation.

125

I try to make people aware of how dangerous mania is. A person in a full blown manic episode does not have solid judgment or control over their behavior. Not only can it be destructive to relationships and the sufferer's financial situation, it can lead to risks to their lives and to the lives of others. "I wish I had your energy!" I often heard. *No, you don't! I can't control my life!*

The other "manic baptisms" were similar in nature. A burning high would lead to a paroxysm of insight. Falsely so, in my opinion, I would see at a later time. In my spiritual walk, I try to evaluate the validity of the experience by comparing the insights I achieve to what I normally accept as true and within the bounds of reasonable thinking. If it is too conservative or lacking in good moral judgment, I re-evaluate my position in a time when my mind is more controlled and my behavior more disciplined by common sense. It is difficult for a person with or without a mental illness to distinguish which beliefs are based on superstition and which are spiritual beliefs which, though they cannot necessarily be proved at this point in time scientifically, are assumptions that logically follow one's beliefs and experience. Meditation, prayer, and worship, I believe can lead us to a higher understanding of that innate light that is around, through, and within us. I know that we are healed mentally and spiritually by our faith. It has also been shown scientifically that prayer and meditation affect positively the health and mental state, even when the person who is the subject of prayer is not aware that prayer has been offered for them. I saw my cat pawing at a spot of light on the wall. She was frustrated because she could not grasp it. She scratched and pawed, but the light could not be contained. This is, in fact how I experience the Light of God, if you will. It cannot be displayed or is not something we can materially examine. It is an inward looking, taking a leap of faith, into something that is beyond our comprehension. We can be vessels of that light in our physical bodies, but the Spirit of God, cannot be defined in human language, but merely is. I believe that very Light has led me out of Dark Night of the Soul I entered as I gave up custody of my daughter. Without a doubt, honestly looking at questions of whether having this belief or that belief can lead us in the process of being transformed to be more like the Light. What is important to me is what I have seen and experienced, that the seeking of that Light leads to mental and spiritual health and healing, and a hardening of the heart to that Light leads to despair and cynicism.

I felt that I could not adequately care for my daughter. For several years, she went back and forth from her home with her father and stepmother to her home with me. I had to decide what was best for her. I felt extreme guilt and shame. I grieved. It was as though she had died. I could no longer hold her in my lap. The thought of her growing up without me ripped my heart into shreds. Much of the time I would have rather been dead.

I went in and out of hospitals. Once I was restrained in a bed for eight days because I could not promise not to hurt myself. Meals were brought to me, and I was allowed a shower each day. I am now seldom bored for I learned to entertain myself with my imagination and thought processes. The blank walls in the seclusion rooms where I spent many a day contained the projections of imaginary dialogues, replays of past events, and anticipations of future events. Because of this sort of training of my mind, I seldom get bored when waiting for an appointment or am at home alone. I do not ever have the T.V. on when I am home alone. Rather, I am stretching and exercising my thinking processes. Later, as I began to do meditation as a spiritual practice, this became very useful.

I think the most tragic part of this decade was a loss of connection with the community at large. There is a subculture of the mentally ill who are under treatment. This is both beneficial and harmful. It furthers the focus on the stigma, symptoms, and self-image of the mentally ill. Suicide, of course, to give an example, occurs at a larger percentage among the mentally ill. Being part of that subculture to some extent normalizes thinking in terms of suicide and the actual experience of suicide itself. The mentally ill need places where they can freely and without judgment talk about troubling issues. However, I think it is a huge disservice not to reintegrate those in recovery back into the community.

To me mental illness is a form of diversity. Do we merely allow those with such a diversity to remain equal but separate? Is this not the basis of segregation? It is fought against in other diverse groups, why not among the mentally ill? I do not believe in the concept of mental illness existing as a separate disorder. It can be thought of in terms of brain dysfunction. It can be dealt with on the level of experience, behavior, biology, genetics, sociological issues, chemistry. To be pragmatic, all avenues have a place in treatment of "mental illness." I think it interesting that science, which declines to claim scientific proof for the mind, is the very instrument used for treating so called "mental illness." Interestingly, when a disease like Alzheimer's of Parkinson's disease shows a physiological component that is visible, it moves from the classification of mental illness to a brain disorder. Do we only believe what we see? Do we not have faith in what will be discovered? The mind all of us know has a real existence, and a very powerful one. It is not separate, however, from the brain. We are incarnated as humans in a tangible body. Our minds and bodies are not split, as long as we inhabit that body. A mental illness must not be thought of as shameful, but as a complex disorder of components such as thought, existential components, behavior, anatomical, physiological, and developmental and conditioned responses.

And here, I preach to myself. Much cruelty was inflicted upon me, quite frequently from the only source to which I looked for comfort, the mental health system. I can remember the professional rape I experienced at the hands of one of the residents at the old Louisville General Hospital. The only question I have in my mind today is, was it "professional rape," or was it outright assault? Either way, somehow I came out being treated like a whore. After the event, it was suggested I go to North Carolina to be "treated." The perpetrator, perhaps, got a slap on the hand, though I wonder if even that occurred.

This doctor, a doctor from another culture, took a special interest in me and I was flattered. He agreed to come to my home for dinner at 7:00 PM. I cooked steaks on the grill and made side dishes. I had little money and this was a sacrifice for me. 7:15 PM, 7:30 PM, 8:00 PM came and no show. But at 9:00 PM he knocks at the door. The dinner, of course, was ruined, but that was not his interest. He pulls me by the arm and throws me on the bed, and I lay there like a rag doll while he screwed me. The most interesting thing was his statement as he performed this act, "If only DR. X (the attending) could see me now!" What sort of sadistic triumph of power was that?

I went to the only support I thought I had—the hospital. A routine urine test showed a positive pregnancy result. All the staff wanted to know with whom I had been having sex. There was only one—the resident in charge of my care. The patients had a phone that was only for their use. The bastard called me.

"Don't tell anyone about me," he ordered me. "We can take care of this."

"What do you mean, 'take care of this'? For you, or me?"

He hung up.

After his call, I went to my room and started throwing my shoes around. What am I doing with all these shoes? What does he mean, take care of "it"? I hated the world. I despised myself. There is no one I can trust, least of all myself!

My social worker appeared at the door. She implored me to tell her what had happened with me. I simply told her who my sexual partner was. I told her to tell no one. Nothing is a secret between members of a hospital team, however.

As it turns out, because I was on Mellaril, the urine test was a false positive. A blood test confirmed that. I was not pregnant. I didn't see it this way at the time, but the administrative staff had a HUGE problem on their hands. I was unselfishly thinking of what damage I could cause them, and I did not want that. I had a fierce loyalty to anyone I perceived was acting in my best interest. I do not feel to this day that this loyalty was appreciated or acknowledged. Dr. X was an incredibly ethical man and physician, almost a lost breed. He held the patients' confidence in him in the highest regard. I was asked if I wanted to press charges. My one word answer was, "No."

It was suggested I go, with the teachers' insurance I had, to a "beautiful hospital in North Carolina." So I flew with papers given to me from my social worker that described me as some sort of manipulative animal. This reminded me of my mother who said I was "like a little dog that gets kicked and comes back for more."

I left Louisville for North Carolina disillusioned and devastated. No matter what these judgmental professionals thought, suicide was a very real consideration. I was living in fear. Fear of facing the grief of giving up care of my daughter. Fear that there was no real purpose for my existence, and I had to face that. Fear that death would come before I made peace with myself or God. I felt in my deepest despair that the answer was to be a good Christian, but I did not have firm convictions of what that meant for me. Ratting on a lover? Was he a lover?

But, fear is just a door to be opened. In acknowledging my fear, I had, in fact, taken the first step to recovery. It would not be resolved with a few weeks, months or years of experience and therapy. The longer I stood trembling, afraid, staring at that door, the larger and heavier it became. Was there anything on the other side? Clearly, the superstitious side of my Christian beliefs only increased my torment for I continually failed to meet my own expectations.

Great fear would be replaced at times with great anger. I would lash out unexpectedly. Anger would precipitate self-hatred. Self-hatred would precipitate self-destructive acts. Intense grief over my daughter and my life, the loss of my home and career would bring on the desire for self-annihilation. Clearly, my psychiatrist in North Carolina recognized that.

But, no amount of insight or support would stop the self-loathing. I, in addition to all the useless acts of harming myself, decided to hang myself. I went to the bathroom in my room and tied the belt of my bathrobe around my neck, securing it like a noose. I stood on the bathtub with it tight and stepped down. Immediately, the blood flow was cut off from my brain, and I was unconscious. Miraculously, the staff found me before death occurred. I was told my eyes were bulging out when they found me. Once again, I survived.

I was on the acute unit for a long time after that. This acute unit was quite different from those I had experience in other hospitals. There was a limited amount of structured time where we did art or played games. We had various forms of psychotherapy.

The individual rooms were the place where we spent most of our time, however. There were padded walls and floors and a mattress. A window let in light. It was heavily screened. In spite of all these precautions, there were still incidences. One male patient was able to somehow get a cigarette lighter, forbidden on the unit, into his room and set it on fire. I have no speculations on how he obtained it or what his motive was.

The days led to two years at the hospital. I had stopped the burning and cutting while in the hospital, voluntarily requesting to be sent to acute when I felt the anguish was leading me in that direction. An internal question, however, had not been resolved. Was life worth living? My insurance ran out and I was discharged, ill prepared for what still lay ahead. I moved back to Louisville. Shortly after that, I returned to previous behaviors.

An overdose, once again, brought me to a near death. I overdosed on Elavil, an antidepressant with many fatalities on its list for overdose. I knew this. This is why I chose it.

I took a bottle that had just been filled and lay down in my bed in an apartment I had rented. I was alone. I cannot remember anything about being found and transported to the hospital. I had an experience that I opened my eyes and saw a light. I said, "I want to live." I heard applause all around me, and the next thing I knew, I awakened on a critical care unit with a ventilator and tubes everywhere in and out of my body. I was told I had stopped breathing by the time the ambulance got me to the ER. There were other self-destructive acts, other times when I wanted to opt out, but after that decision I got myself to the hospital whenever I was losing a grip on the desire to live.

Eventually, the cutting and burning dwindled away also. The incidents became very far apart and finally disappeared. I was in the ER with a serious burn when I made the decision to stop this behavior. A doctor, standing behind me, said to me, "Why would you want to mutilate yourself that way?"

My response, though I was silent was, "Why would I?" At that moment, I decided to fight this urge to destroy my flesh. I do not know this doctor's name. I do not remember his appearance. It was something he asked at the right moment. I wish I could thank him.

Yet, the frequent hospitalizations continued. I went from hospital to hospital, doctor to doctor, therapist to therapist.

I had what I began to describe as "brain pain," an intense anguish that went beneath any external circumstance. I had lost many friends in the mental health system to suicide. I was working very hard at not letting that be an option, but it was frequently a struggle that drained me, literally, into physical weakness.

One of my greatest blessings was finding Bridgehaven. I had gone there with a group of mental health advocates, discussing the parity of payment for mental health issues as compared to physical issues. We met with the President and C.E.O. of this "clubhouse" for the mentally ill. I was immediately drawn to her because she was frank yet compassionate. She presented to us a list of groups and services provided by the organization.

When I saw the long list of the services provided in this large, open, clean building I said, "I would like to come here."

She leaned over the table, and said, "Lynn, if you would like to come here, we would love to have you." Thus, another piece of hope, another piece in the puzzle fell into place. I soon became a member of Bridgehaven. This marked the beginning of true recovery.

The Liberation of a Moth

I sit on the covered balcony
    looking at the pattern of the Light
    upon the grey painted floor

hidden in the same color
is a moth
    stuck between the splits
    between the wooden boards
    there it was
    a piece of weed holding it back
    hooked onto one of its back legs

                                                        carefully

I touch a tiny piece of
leaf and
free it from its load for
it struggles to fly

free from its burden
it lingers
I imagine it afraid
of the unseen power
a power physically larger
than itself
perhaps so large
it cannot be perceived

I gently nudge it
forward
(did I inflict pain?)

suddenly
it flies
up and over the
metal bars that
guard the balcony

I watch it disappear
into transparent air
and fly away

smaller and smaller
until it is but a dot
then gone
invisible

I ask myself,
"Why do I feel liberated?"

Chapter Eleven

Recovery: An Acceptance of Pain

Our greatest teacher is pain. We strive as living creatures to move away from it. If our hearts are not hardened, we learn. The sword of pain pulls us forward. The acceptance of life—with its joys, hardships, aversions, desires—is the beginning of healing for all of us, mentally ill or not. Fear often stymies us, keeps us locked, frozen, or running. Fear is also only a door. It is the door we must open or we are trapped. Fear of looking at ourselves is one of our biggest obstacles—looking at our flaws, our humanness, and our mortality. First, we see the goldfish in the bowl floating belly up. At some point we realize we, too, will be that fish.

All these fears I walked into my new therapist, Gloria. She always says, "When the student is ready, the teacher is there." And there she was. I was desperate to be completely honest, as much as I was capable about the bottom line truths that had oppressed me. Yet, I did not want to go through my long history of suffering and pain. I wanted a way out.

It was a lengthy process, hard work on both our parts. She was a technician of great practical wisdom. Often spoke with examples from her own life. She and I began with my overwhelming anxiety and mood swings—what could I do to help myself? I could not get through a night without calling a Crisis Hotline! Usually two or three times! I feared that death was imminent, I would have a heart attack or was dying of cancer, yet wanted so much at times to control that by taking my life. It was a paradox—to rid myself of death, I must hasten it.

Gloria arranged for me to alternate weeks between herself and a very gifted art therapist, Jim W. I had a minimal art ability, and Jim would encourage me to develop in technique and composition as well as discussing the emotional and psychological patterns that popped up time and time again in my art.

With Gloria, I learned simple ideas of how to deal with pain—of any sort. For example, often when I felt disorganized and anxious I would organize a small section of my apartment such as the coffee table. I would feel better!

I made lists, and schedules, and index cards to remind me of what I could do when a particularly strong emotion surged. The part of me that was a librarian enjoyed this. I loved scratching things off my list I had accomplished.

Gloria has never "told me what to do." In fact, many a time, when I have been in great pain, she has said, "If I had a magic wand I would wave it over you." It gave me confidence and a sense of self-worth to see real, measurable progress. I was sleeping better and taking better care of my basic needs.

When a crisis would come, I had a saying, "Back to the basics." Taking care of my basic needs like eating and resting were to be my number one priority when things seemed to crumble around me.

I learned to change my thoughts when I was fearful. Do something practical. Make a conscious decision to change a behavior that was causing me distress. I began to see that changing my behavior also changed the way I felt.

I really liked what Bridgehaven had to offer in general. There was the "open door" policy, meaning, unless a clinical worker needed privacy for a member or was in a meeting or individual session, there door was open. They used the same restrooms we did. This may sound idiotic, but in the clinical settings I had been in, restrooms were segregated; there were the staff restrooms and the patient restrooms. It is a reminder of the way things were for African Americans before the Civil Rights movements. All this chiseled away at the misconception that staff had something, and were something, that the clients, patients, mentally ill could not consider as equal to what they were as people. In fact, Gloria repeatedly reminded me that "no one just falls into this profession."

The most significant, the most healing, gift that I received was that the staff at Bridgehaven LIKED ME. I had been much maligned by frustrated mental health professionals in the past. Not that I do not understand how repetitive self-destructive behavior could become intolerable, but I always was treated as though I were playing a game, when in fact, I was desperately trying to find a reason why I should change my behavior or why I even deserved their respect. I made it worse by increasing the severity of the acts over time. I wanted someone to tell me it was not my fault I was mentally ill. Yet, I had not reached the point where I saw responsible action as the Solution.

At Bridgehaven with Jim W's encouragement I became an avid artist. Not only did I show and sell art at Bridgehaven, I had art shows across the city. One of my pieces hangs in Frankfort, Kentucky, the state capital, in The Department of Protection and Advocacy. One is in Tucson Arizona at the office of C.A.R.F. Both were purchased and hung in the offices.

Having always had the ethic of expressing gratitude, when Bridgehaven lost funding from the Louisville Metro Government, I personally got petitions from fifty Bridgehaven members and spoke in front of the council with the CEO of Bridgehaven. The funding was restored. It was the influence of Bridgehaven, not just on myself, but an attitude of kindness and compassion towards all members, that gave me a great desire to advocate for them. We were called members, not patients or clients.

I was an institutionalized individual. Gloria did not push me to give up that role. I had to achieve that further down the road. The institutional life had given me security, and a kind of wall with which to hit the balls of doubt and fear and see in what direction they landed. However, we did discuss, often, the role of institutional life and the gain I did or did not receive from it. As for an intervention for safety, it was of course actually encouraged.

While Gloria was practical and pragmatic, Jim W. was more conceptual. We discussed through art therapy the roles different parts of my personality played in my survival. I then could make a more conscious, logical decision as to the current effectiveness that part played and choose whether to hang on to it or ditch it. It was never threatening, for what Jim and Gloria both did was mentor me in the path of self-discovery.

I also had a difficulty tolerating medications and establishing effective doses without a great deal of side effects. After being at Bridgehaven for a while, I went less frequently to the hospital and would go for a crisis stay at Wellspring Crisis Stabilization Unit (C.S.U.). Here there were clinical staff, and a psychiatrist, who could better monitor the effects of medication and other forms of therapy in an environment that was not like a psychiatric unit in the hospital. There was much more freedom, and a more relaxed relationship between staff and residents. The stay was generally brief, five to ten days or so. Instead of 20 to 30 clients, as in hospitals, there were usually 6 to 8. Individual counseling was a big part of the treatment process there. Bridgehaven worked closely with C.S.U.

Still there was a bondage with institutional life. What was missing? I could not rid myself of the obsession of death, and my own insignificance as an individual. I think in the hospital I dealt with raw survival. The control of staff over patients was the object of my rebellion. I wanted to somehow get around it, find a way of dealing with it, or end its dominance over my life completely. I focused on the war, not the ideology of the war.

One of the hardest lessons I learned by reflecting on my life and what I learned in therapy and through contemplation, was that not all people had my best interest at heart—in the hospital or out of it. I questioned whether everything happened for good. What I decided was that no, definitely not all things that had happened to me in this world were for my good, or the good of anyone. BUT ALL THINGS, if we do not harden our hearts, can teach us hard, hard lessons, and in that way work together for our good. Our suffering is painful. We can learn from it. We do not have to accept it as a "good thing" that happened to us or what we brought on ourselves was a "good thing." But, we can be thankful for the lessons learned.

"I CAN'T HELP MYSELF!" I often screamed. However, we must never, ever negate the importance of responsible action. I began to make responsible actions working with Gloria. A person viewing the small, seemingly insignificant victories, might think of them as small, insignificant victories. However, with the mentally ill, something as insignificant as brushing one's teeth might be a mountain climbed. The changing of one's thinking was shown to me to be critical in the way one acted.

I have experienced depression so intense that getting out of bed to even go to the bathroom seemed an almost impossible feat. I would have to pray for the ability. I would have to visualize myself getting up, getting a glass of water, going to the bathroom. Emotional pain can be as debilitating as physical pain.

I remember a conversation with Lynda, when she asked, not in a confronting way, it was obvious, but as though she really wanted to understand,

"Why would a person not get out of bed, knowing getting out of bed would make them less depressed. Let's say you were, on a scale of one to ten with one being not depressed and ten being suicidal, a nine. You knew getting out of bed would lower it to seven, why would you not get out of bed?"

"You just feel that it is all but impossible," came my answer.

"But, if there was a fire, you would get out of bed."

"Have you ever had the flu, Lynda?"

"No, I haven't."

"But, you have been so sick you felt you could not get out of bed?"

"Yes."

"But," I pursued this line of explanation, "if there was a fire you would get out of bed."

"Yes."

"Severe depression is no different. It zaps your energy and motivation."

"Your energy and motivation…"

The conversation changed then to a different subject. I don't know if the question was resolved in her mind.

I worked on these basic skills with Gloria. I would make a list of three things I was going to accomplish in a day and feel rewarded when they were done. Her patience and understanding of this still astounds me. She believes in the power of cognitive therapy, and I, also, have seen its fruits.

I started to break through the spiritual component of my illness on a trip to the hospital, ironically where this story began—at the state mental hospital. I had gone to the E.R. in one of my deep, deep depressions. I could not care for myself, and I knew it.

In the emergency psychiatry department I lay on one of the beds in the back where they had put me until I could be admitted to a hospital. The resident who had interviewed me, though I do not remember his name, I can remember was quite compassionate. As I lay there, unable to even lift my head when I was addressed, he came to me and said, "We are sending you to the state hospital."

With all the horrors this brought to mind of the way the hospital had been decades and decades ago, I said, "No. I don't want to go there."

"With symptoms like yours, I cannot let you go home. Hopefully, it won't be a long stay. We have called every hospital in the city, and there are no other beds."

I was too depressed to respond. I knew it would be to no avail, anyway. I resigned myself to accept this fact, and, hopefully be able to pull my wits together enough to get out quickly. I knew they had a different building and that the stays did not generally last for months and months.

I was transported by ambulance, and the admission process was started. The admitting doctor was a gentle woman. My clothes were searched and any strings attached were cut off with my permission, or the article was put aside until I was released. I was offered a processed turkey sandwich on thin white bread, which I accepted without enthusiasm.

The unit, though comfortable, bore, like myself the marks of aging—worn scratches in the surfaces around the nurses' station, like the old scars on my arms and legs, chips in the marbled linoleum, worn paint on the walls. Men were on one end of the unit, and women on the other. There were two community areas, one with a T.V. and comfortable chairs, and one with tables and chairs for eating, socializing and playing cards.

There was an exit leading to the main hallway, and an exit to an area that was central to all the units around it. It was used to take patients out every hour to smoke or simply get a breath of air. I found out many patients actually requested this hospital because of the smoke breaks that were allowed.

In my first session with my psychiatrist, he inquired about my mood. Though more interested in simply getting out, I answered truthfully I was very depressed.

He asked, "What has got you so depressed?" He sounded sincere.

"Life is full of pain and suffering," I blandly, honestly answered.

"THAT," he said with authority," is the first tenant of Buddhism"

I looked at him in disbelief. He did not try to make me put on different glasses. He did not dispute me. He did not talk about the beauty of life or tell me this view was indicative of my depression. Buddhism . . . I would have to look into this.

The days passed quickly, and I returned to muddling through life, and trying to use my "coping skills" to manage the symptoms. Life did seem to be better for a while, but I had the extreme mood swings and also suffered intense anxiety. Gloria worked with me and Jim helped me get on ground with my art.

Progress definitely had been made. I just couldn't quite put together the puzzle with missing pieces. I was on a lot of medication—two of which were highly addictive. In reading on addiction I came across an article about Buddhism. The Second Noble Truth, as it was called was described as, "The cause of suffering is craving, in all its forms—addiction, clinging, desire, aversion."

"Wow!" I thought, "That is the cause of my suffering. I want this. I either get it or I don't. If I do get it, I am happy for a while, but it doesn't last. If I don't get it I feel suffering because I WANT IT! I CRAVE IT!" I read further.

"There is relief from suffering," I read further as the article stated a Third Noble Truth.

The Fourth Noble Truth was the solution to suffering, The Noble Eightfold Path. I made a decision to rid myself of my addictions. I did not begin to understand all the nuances of this way of life—the awareness of delusional thought (false belief), the need for mindfulness and discipline, and the nature of reality as an impermanent object, for example. I did not see how greatly my life would be changed as I began the practice of Buddhism.

Beginning on the most superficial level, I decided to rid myself of the addictive drugs. To help me with that, I began Insight Meditation, as best I could as I understood it from my research. I immediately was able to let go of one of my obsessions: the need to be recognized. All the approval I had sought, all of it was pointless. There would never be enough recognition if I made this the goal of my life. Somehow, I thought if I could be recognized as a writer, an artist or "a something," I would gain freedom from death. But, I asked myself, how many people must recognize me? Is one other person enough? A nation? The world? It was a bottomless well! The world would change, and my recognition would more than likely end or be of insignificance.

I started reading voraciously. I was emailing a Buddhist teacher who did not at first respond—no doubt picking up on the still glaring symptoms of my mental illness. But, at last the center where he was located did, in fact, respond, and I was referred to a local sangha, a group of disciplined meditators.

In the meantime I had checked myself into C.S.U. to get off of some of this intense medication that kept me hazy and lacking in clear perception of what was around me. With meditation I had begun the process, but needed objective observation of my progress. As a cautionary note, medications withdrawal should be supervised by a health professional.

The psychiatrist there encouraged me, and saw this as progress. He was himself a Buddhist! He said he had never seen me so calm and happy. There was definitely a spiritual awakening, but years of practice showed me one does not stop with initial awareness. Transformation takes root and builds over time.

I continued in my Buddhist practice, after I left C.S.U., and continue to this day. Perhaps I do not see my life as groundless anymore, though. I eventually came to resolve any conflict I had with my faith in God and the very practical applications of Buddhism. Meditation brought me focus, is bringing me freedom from my addictions, and is bringing me awareness of myself. I live peacefully most of the time. My life is disciplined. I have put great effort into my Buddhist practice. I stop when I feel a symptom that is a distraction from my practice and "sit with it." I even have sat with hallucinations screaming at me and accepted that they were there but were merely distractions from my practice. Still, I cannot give up my roots! In a moment when I perceive danger, I call for God to help me. He is the strength when I am weak. It is not impossible to mesh the philosophy of giving up on the idea of the permanence of reality with a belief that there is something even bigger than impermanence. The Light that was bigger than the desire to destroy myself was always there, that which is within us all, I believe. I was, at first fearful of what the Buddhists call the Heavenly Messengers, the sickness, old age and death, that always face us in this life. Yet, admitting they were there and I could not escape that reality, at some point brought me acceptance of the inevitability of the end of our life on Earth. Facing of reality and the acceptance by faith of a spirit that was larger than any questions I might have, or debates with my own conscience, brought me mental health. I could think of death for the most part as a reminder to stay in this point of time right here, this moment and live it to its fullest. My desire to worship God, the Creator, the all in all, and the great joy in feeling the sacred ground on which, I believe, we always stand, let me stay in this moment without fear.

The second person who came into my life who challenged every belief I had, pushing me to define my faith I have, was and is my friend Stuart. Stuart and I do not and never did have a romantic relationship. Our personalities are quite different, but we can spend hours talking of our perceptions and beliefs and the Truth or delusional nature of those perceptions and beliefs. We challenge each other, which I see has helped me understand through doubting. We discuss the chaos of our minds and thoughts, and how they sometimes come together as an insight. Then that insight falls through the box in which we have put it and we pick it up and arrange the pieces in a different form.

I found as I became more independent in my thinking, I did not depend on other people as much to be my conscience. I chose what I believed to be right or wrong. I chose what I thought was the meaning of compassion was. The Buddha said, "Be a lamp unto yourself."

It freed me to be more accepting of other people's beliefs. My path has led me here. The road that others followed was something between them and God. My Buddhist beliefs had helped me let go of people, and let them figure out what meaning they found in their journey. My faith in a loving God allowed me to believe in the grace that power extended, to learn how to live joyfully in the face of those Heavenly Messengers, to ease my grip on what I, if I was honest, had believed was all I had, my life as an individual separate from the Great Oneness. I no longer wanted to follow mankind like the wind, down this path or that. It was my life, my choice how I reacted to an ever-changing universe. We do not live in an ideal world. I mean ideal in the sense that it is the way we want it to be. "Perfect does not exist. Every human is different. Equations are not linear. Absolutely nothing meets the ideal. Yet, we are all created perfect, diverse, but perfect in our own right. The idea of "right or wrong," or "good and bad" exists in a grey zone—in fact such ideals do not exist but yet are there! It's all right here, right now. This is the perfect moment.

One significant change was that I no longer wanted someone to teach, and I no longer wanted to follow. I had no desire to be a leader, the top Buddhist or the great Christian. I have always known we all stand naked in front of God. It is like we are a painting hiding from the artist. Just as I am is how I am seen. I realized all I have to offer is my presence through deep, deep listening. Even with our fellow humans, we may try to hide our foibles, but somehow they always show. Why do we pretend? Why does fear keep us from showing what is already known? Just as I am. This love and acceptance of ourselves enables us to reach to others in kindness and acceptance. Honesty about what we feel or have felt is a beautiful gift for someone special. Or, even for the clerk behind the desk. Our clumsiness becomes more acceptable to us. We are less ashamed.

I was asked by Stuart if our beliefs could keep us from awakening. Does the belief the sun will rise keep morning coming? So much we believe that we have not seen. I cannot in peace believe that behind the door there is nothing. Yet, to find the Truth we must constantly seek it. Where is the sword pointing? The answer is where? Do not be afraid of calling a table a table, even though we know eventually it will be rotten wood. Inevitably.

Neither be afraid of the Darkness of the mind. It consumes nothing, but lets the Light shine. Thoughts, perceptions, feelings, mental formations are as meteors and distant stars against a dark sky. Or perhaps the rainbow after a thunderous rain.

I Will Be Your Voice
Song of Bridgehaven

Shriveled Man, picking up
Butts off the courtyard floor, picking
Up tobacco to roll into self-engineered
Cigarettes to inhale with desperation

I will be your voice

I will be your voice, Child Like Woman,
Speaking in
Similes
As though a direct asking of
Your needs would
Burn your soul,

Cowering Woman,
I will be your voice when
The thunderous rain beats you as
Surely as the violent man
Who calls himself your lover.

I will be your voice when
The sun scorches your
Crisp face and your constant
Walking tires your swollen

Ankles. Your fear keeps you
Wandering to the hospital lobbies, or,
Perhaps even the jails.
I curse the illness that keeps
You terrified of anyone who

Gives you a sidelong glance.

I am your voice,
Those who sit at the table with
Me, bearing wrinkled hearts, bearing
Devastated hope lost (is it possible to regain?)

I cannot stop the
Hail which pounds from some
Unknown power.
I cannot sweep the shredded
Rug of sleet or
The quiet,

But deadly to the homeless,
Snow. But,

I will be your voice.
*   —Lynn Nackson*

www.ingramcontent.com/pod-product-compliance
Lightning Source LLC
Chambersburg PA
CBHW070655290526
45790CB00001B/328